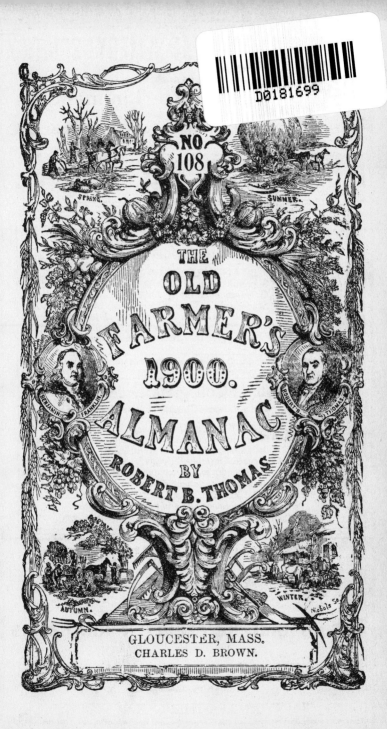

NO 108

SPRING

SUMMER

THE
OLD
FARMER'S
1900.
ALMANAC

BENJAMIN FRANKLIN

ROBERT B. THOMAS

BY
ROBERT B. THOMAS

AUTUMN

WINTER

Nichols Sc

GLOUCESTER, MASS.
CHARLES D. BROWN.

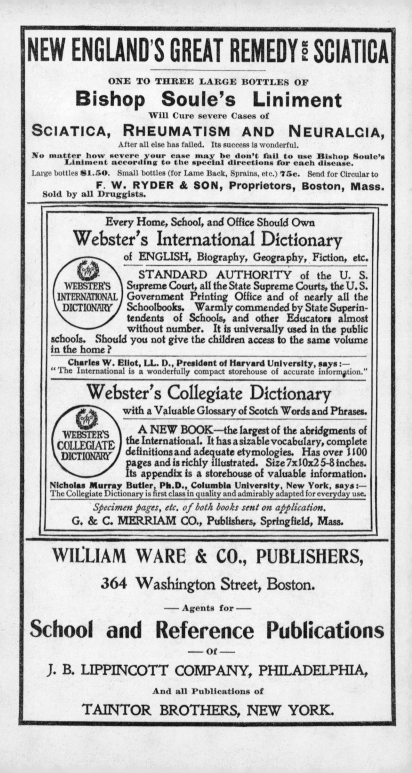

THE
(OLD)
FARMER'S ALMANACK,

CALCULATED ON A NEW AND IMPROVED PLAN
FOR THE YEAR OF OUR LORD

1900

Being 4th after BISSEXTILE or LEAP-YEAR, and (until July 4)
124th of American Independence.

FITTED FOR BOSTON, BUT WILL ANSWER FOR ALL THE NEW ENGLAND STATES.

Containing, beside the large number of Astronomical Calculations,
and the Farmer's Calendar for every month
in the year, a variety of

NEW, USEFUL, AND ENTERTAINING MATTER.

ESTABLISHED IN 1793,

BY ROBERT B. THOMAS.

Hark! hark! the music of the chime!
The King is dead! God's blessing on the King!
Welcome with gladness this new King of Time.
MRS. AUGUSTA WEBSTER.

BOSTON:
PUBLISHED BY WILLIAM WARE & CO.

Sold by Booksellers and Traders throughout New England.

TO PATRONS AND CORRESPONDENTS.

To our readers and friends we present the " Old Farmer's Almanack " for the year 1900. It will be observed that there is an addition to its number of pages, and a consequent re-arrangement of subjects. To enable one to promptly find any desired information we have inserted below a list of contents. We trust that our readers will find this number of solid value, and that they will realize in full measure all the benefits from the material herein furnished which it is our earnest desire to bestow.

" It is by our works and not by our words we would be judged: these we hope will sustain us in the humble though proud station we have so long held. . . .

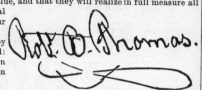

CONTENTS.

JANUARY.

S	M	T	W	Th	F	S
-	1	2	3	4	5	6
7	8	9	10	11	12	13
14	15	16	17	18	19	20
21	22	23	24	25	26	27
28	29	30	31	-	-	-
-	-	-	-	-	-	-

FEBRUARY.

S	M	T	W	Th	F	S
-	-	-	-	1	2	3
4	5	6	7	8	9	10
11	12	13	14	15	16	17
18	19	20	21	22	23	24
25	26	27	28	-	-	-
-	-	-	-	-	-	-

MARCH.

S	M	T	W	Th	F	S
-	-	-	-	1	2	3
4	5	6	7	8	9	10
11	12	13	14	15	16	17
18	19	20	21	22	23	24
25	26	27	28	29	30	31
-	-	-	-	-	-	-

APRIL.

S	M	T	W	Th	F	S
1	2	3	4	5	6	7
8	9	10	11	12	13	14
15	16	17	18	19	20	21
22	23	24	25	26	27	28
29	30	-	-	-	-	-
-	-	-	-	-	-	-

MAY.

S	M	T	W	Th	F	S
-	-	1	2	3	4	5
6	7	8	9	10	11	12
13	14	15	16	17	18	19
20	21	22	23	24	25	26
27	28	29	30	31	-	-
-	-	-	-	-	-	-

JUNE.

S	M	T	W	Th	F	S
-	-	-	-	-	1	2
3	4	5	6	7	8	9
10	11	12	13	14	15	16
17	18	19	20	21	22	23
24	25	26	27	28	29	30
-	-	-	-	-	-	-

JULY.

S	M	T	W	Th	F	S
1	2	3	4	5	6	7
8	9	10	11	12	13	14
15	16	17	18	19	20	21
22	23	24	25	26	27	28
29	30	31	-	-	-	-
-	-	-	-	-	-	-

AUGUST.

S	M	T	W	Th	F	S
-	-	-	1	2	3	4
5	6	7	8	9	10	11
12	13	14	15	16	17	18
19	20	21	22	23	24	25
26	27	28	29	30	31	-
-	-	-	-	-	-	-

SEPTEMBER.

S	M	T	W	Th	F	S
-	-	-	-	-	-	1
2	3	4	5	6	7	8
9	10	11	12	13	14	15
16	17	18	19	20	21	22
23	24	25	26	27	28	29
30	-	-	-	-	-	-

OCTOBER.

S	M	T	W	Th	F	S
-	1	2	3	4	5	6
7	8	9	10	11	12	13
14	15	16	17	18	19	20
21	22	23	24	25	26	27
28	29	30	31	-	-	-
-	-	-	-	-	-	-

NOVEMBER.

S	M	T	W	Th	F	S
-	-	-	-	1	2	3
4	5	6	7	8	9	10
11	12	13	14	15	16	17
18	19	20	21	22	23	24
25	26	27	28	29	30	-
-	-	-	-	-	-	-

DECEMBER.

S	M	T	W	Th	F	S
-	-	-	-	-	-	1
2	3	4	5	6	7	8
9	10	11	12	13	14	15
16	17	18	19	20	21	22
23	24	25	26	27	28	29
30	31	-	-	-	-	-

EXPLANATIONS FOR CALENDAR PAGES.

The **Calculations** are made in *Standard Time* (i.e., the time of the 75th meridian West from Greenwich), 16 min. behind Boston time, for the longitude and latitude of Boston, and for general purposes are sufficiently accurate for all parts of New England. If, however, greater accuracy is desired, the following precepts can be regarded.

The Table given below contains corrections for the principal cities of the New England States; and any other place in New England can use the correction of the place in the Table which is nearest in longitude to itself.

For Sun Fast, subtract tabular quantity if longitude from Boston is West, but add it if East. For Moon Souths add tabular quantity if longitude is West, but subtract it if East.

For the Rising and Setting of the Sun, Moon, and Planets add tabular quantity if longitude from Boston is West, but subtract if East; and this will give the correct value when the place is in or near the same latitude as Boston. When the place differs considerably in latitude from that of Boston, the correction will also be right when the celestial body is on or near the equator, and when it is remote from the equator this corrected result will still be approximately right.

	East.		*West.*		*West.*
Augusta, Me.	. . . 5 min.	Keene, N. H..	. . . 5 min.	Williamstown, Mass.	9 min.
Portland, Me.	. . . 3 "	Montpelier, Vt.	. . 6 "	Newport, R. I.	. . 1 "
Biddeford, Me.	. . . 2 "	Brattleboro, Vt.	. . 6 "	Providence, R. I.	. . 1 "
Portsmouth, N.H.	. . 1 "	Burlington, Vt.	. . 9 "	New London, Conn.	. . 4 "
Provincetown, Mass.	4 "	Lowell, Mass.	. . . 1 "	Hartford, Conn.	. . 7 "
	West.	Worcester, Mass..	. 3 "	New Haven, Conn.	. 7 "
Concord, N. H.	. . . 2 min.	Springfield, Mass.	. 6 "	Bridgeport, Conn..	. 9 "

MORNING AND EVENING STARS.

The inferior planets are Evening Stars from superior to inferior conjunction, and Morning Stars from inferior to superior conjunction.

The superior planets are Evening Stars from opposition to conjunction, and Morning Stars from conjunction to opposition.

JULIAN PERIOD.

The Julian Period is a cycle of 7980 years, and is used by astronomers and chronologists as a convenient method of reckoning the interval between dates, and also as a means of expressing chronological eras.

The present period began at noon of Jan. 1, 4713 B.C. so that over 1300 years must still elapse before it is ended, and then another period will begin.

TIDE TABLE.

The tides in the Calendar pages are for the port of Boston, in *Standard Time.* The following table contains the approximate difference between the time of High Water at Boston and places named. The reader is warned that this table will not always give the exact time of the tide, as the difference varies from day to day. It is hoped, however, it will be near enough to be useful.

The difference, if preceded by +, is to be added to, or if preceded by —, subtracted from, the time as given in the Calendar pages.

	h. m.		h. m.		h. m.
Baltimore, Md.	. . + 7 30	New Bedford. Mass.	— 3 30	Portsmouth, N. H..	. — 0 06
Bath, Me.	. . + 0 44	Newburyport, Mass.	— 0 07	Salem, Mass.	. . . . — 0 16
Beaufort, N. C.	. — 4 06	Newcastle, Del.	. . + 0 29	Sandy Hook, N. Y.	. — 3 58
Bridgeport, Conn.	. — 0 18	New Haven. Conn.	. — 0 13	Savan'h, Ga., Dry D'k	— 3 16
Cape Henry, Va.	. — 3 34	New London, Conn.	— 2 06	St. Augustine, Fla.	. — 3 08
Cape May, N.J..	. — 3 10	Newport, R. I.	. . — 3 44	Stonington, Conn.	. — 2 22
Charleston. S. C.	. — 4 05	New Rochelle, N.Y.	— 0 07	Viney'd Haven, Mass.	+ 0 14
City Point, Va..	. + 3 08	New York, Gov. Isl.	— 3 22	Washington, D. C.,	
Cold Spring, N. J.	. — 3 57	Norfolk, Va..	. . . — 2 16	Navy Yard	. . . . + 8 41
Eastport. Me.	. . — 0 21	Philadelphia, Pa..	. + 2 15	West Point, N. Y..	. — 0 27
Edgartown, Mass.	. + 0 47	Plymouth, Mass.	. — 0 10	Wilmington, Del.	. . — 2 23
Key West. Fla..	. — 1 59	Point Judith, R. I.	. — 3 57	Wood's Hole, N. side.	— 3 36
Nantucket, Mass.	. + 0 55	Portland, Me.	. . — 0 12	Wood's Hole. S. side.	— 2 53

STANDARD TIME IN CUBA, PORTO RICO, AND THE PHILIPPINES.

By order of the War Department standard time has been established in the territory under government by the military forces of the United States, and all departments under such military government have been directed to officially observe the time furnished by the United States Signal Service as standard time as follows: —

For Cuba, 75th meridian (West Longitude) time;

For Porto Rico, 60th meridian (West Longitude) time;

For the islands of the Philippine Archipelago, 120th meridian (East Longitude) time.

Therefore, according to the standard time prescribed as above, when it is six o'clock a.m. in Boston it will be, —

Six o'clock a.m. in Cuba.

Seven o'clock a.m. in Porto Rico.

Seven o'clock p.m. in the Philippines.

ECLIPSES FOR THE YEAR 1900.

There will be three eclipses this year, two of the SUN and one of the MOON.

I. A TOTAL ECLIPSE OF THE SUN, May 28; visible in New England as a Partial Eclipse. The path of totality passes through Virginia and the south eastern part of the United States, while the northern limit of the eclipse is about the North Pole and the southern limit in the northern part of South America.

Begins, 7h. 53.0m. A.M. *Middle*, 9h. 7.4m. A.M. *Ends* 10h. 29.8m. A.M.

II. A PARTIAL ECLIPSE OF THE MOON, June 12; visible in New England.

Begins, 10h. 24.4m. P.M. *Middle*, 10h. 28.1m. P.M. *Ends*, 10h. 31.7m. P.M.

III. AN ANNULAR ECLIPSE OF THE SUN, Nov. 21 and 22; invisible in New England, but visible as an Annular Eclipse in the southern part of Africa and the western part of Australia

Chronological Cycles for 1900.

Dominical Letter . .	G	Lunar Cycle or Golden Number	1	Year of Roman Indiction.	13
Epact, 29 | Solar Cycle,	5			Year of Julian Period	6613

Movable Feasts and Fasts for 1900.

Septuagesima Su.,	Feb. 11	Good Friday,	Apr. 13	Whit-Sunday,	June 3
Shrove Sunday,	" 25	Easter Sunday,	" 15	Corpus Christi,	" 7
Ash Wednesday,	" 28	Low Sunday,	" 22	Trinity Sunday,	" 10
1st Sunday in Lent.	Mar. 4	Rogation Sunday,	May 20	Advent Sunday,	Dec. 2
Palm Sunday,	Apr. 8	Holy Thursday,	" 24		

PLANETS 1900.

JANUARY.		D.	h.	m.	
Venus	♀ sets	4	6	35	P.M.
Mars	♂ sets	11	4	33	P.M.
Jupiter	♃ rises	19	3	16	A.M.
Saturn	♄ rises	26	4	49	A.M.

FEBRUARY.	D.	h.	m.	
♀ sets	4	7	53	P.M.
♂ rises	12	6	36	A.M.
♃ rises	19	1	35	A.M.
♄ rises	26	2	59	A.M.

MARCH.	D.	h.	m.	
♀ sets	4	8	59	P.M.
♂ rises	12	5	40	A.M.
♃ rises	18	11	54	P.M.
♄ rises	26	1	15	A.M.

APRIL.	D.	h.	m.	
♀ sets	4	10	8	P.M.
♂ rises	12	4	32	A.M.
♃ rises	18	9	49	P.M.
♄ rises	25	11	14	P.M.

MAY.	D.	h.	m.	
♀ sets	4	10	46	P.M.
♂ rises	12	3	26	A.M.
♃ rises	18	7	36	P.M.
♄ rises	25	9	11	P.M.

JUNE.	D.	h.	m.	
♀ sets	4	10	7	P.M.
♂ rises	12	2	22	A.M.
♃ sets	19	2	49	A.M.
♄ sets	26	4	12	A.M.

JULY.	D.	h.	m.	
♀ sets	4	7	28	P.M.
♂ rises	12	1	31	A.M.
♃ sets	19	0	44	A.M.
♄ sets	26	2	5	A.M.

AUGUST.	D.	h.	m.	
♀ rises	5	2	15	A.M.
♂ rises	12	0	50	A.M.
♃ sets	18	10	43	P.M.
♄ sets	25	11	58	P.M.

SEPTEMBER.	D.	h.	m.	
♀ rises	5	1	31	A.M.
♂ rises	12	0	20	A.M.
♃ sets	18	8	51	P.M.
♄ sets	25	9	57	P.M.

OCTOBER.	D.	h.	m.	
♀ rises	5	1	55	P.M.
♂ rises	11	11	51	P.M.
♃ sets	18	7	10	P.M.
♄ sets	25	8	6	P.M.

NOVEMBER.	D.	h.	m.	
♀ rises	5	2	50	A.M.
♂ rises	11	11	12	P.M.
♃ sets	18	5	31	P.M.
♄ sets	25	6	17	P.M.

DECEMBER.	D.	h.	m.	
♀ rises	5	3	56	A.M.
♂ rises	11	10	15	P.M.
♃ rises	19	6	50	A.M.
♄ sets	25	4	34	P.M.

Morning and Evening Stars.

Venus will be Evening Star till July 8, then Morning Star the rest of the year.

Mars will be Evening Star till Jan. 15, then Morning Star the rest of the year.

Jupiter will be Morning Star till May 27, Evening Star till Dec. 14, then Morning Star the rest of the year.

Saturn will be Morning Star till June 23, Evening Star till Dec. 29, then Morning Star the rest of the year.

Names and Characters of the Principal Planets.

●☽○☾ The Moon.	♀ Venus.	⊕ The Earth.	♅ Uranus.	⚵ Juno.
⊙ The Sun.	♂ Mars.	♄ Saturn.	♆ Neptune.	⚴ Pallas.
☿ Mercury.	♃ Jupiter.		⚶ Vesta.	⚳ Ceres.

Names and Characters of the Aspects.

☌ Conjunction, or in the same degree.	☍ Opposition, or 180 degrees.
⚹ Sextile, 60 degrees.	☊ Dragon's Head, or Ascending Node.
□ Quartile, 90 deg. | △ Trine, 120 deg.	☋ Dragon's Tail, or Descending Node.

Names and Characters of the Signs of the Zodiac.

1. ♈ Aries, head.	5. ♌ Leo, heart.	9. ♐ Sagittarius, thighs.
2. ♉ Taurus, neck.	6. ♍ Virgo, belly.	10. ♑ Capricornus, knees.
3. ♊ Gemini, arms.	7. ♎ Libra, reins.	11. ♒ Aquarius, legs.
4. ♋ Cancer, breast	8. ♏ Scorpio, secrets.	12. ♓ Pisces, feet.

UNITED STATES DEPARTMENT OF AGRICULTURE.

Weather Bureau.

Chief of Weather Bureau, Willis L. Moore, Washington, D. C.
Local Forecast Official and Director for New England Section, John W. Smith, Post Office Building, Boston.
Stations and Officials in Charge in the New England Section:

Boston, Mass., John W. Smith, Local Forecast Official;
Block Island, R. I.. Walter L. Day, Observer;
Eastport, Me., Daniel C. Murphy, Observer;
Nantucket, Mass., William W. Neifert, Observer;
Narragansett Pier, R.I., Mrs. Mary E. Conway, Observer;

New Haven, Conn., Leonard M. Tarr, Observer;
Northfield, Vt., William A. Shaw, Observer;
Portland, Me., Edward P. Jones, Observer;
Vineyard Haven, Mass., Henry B. Dick, Observer;
Woods Hole, Mass., Albert J. Davis, Observer.

Officials in charge of stations will, in answer to inquiry by mail, telegraph or telephone, state weather conditions and prospects; any expenses attending the transmission of messages to be paid by the person making inquiry.

WEATHER SIGNALS.

Fair Weather, Rain or Snow, and Temperature Signals. No. 1. A square white flag alone, indicates fair weather, stationary temperature. No. 2. A square blue flag alone, indicates rain or snow, stationary temperature. No. 3. A square white and blue flag (parallel bars of white and blue, the white above the blue) alone, indicates local rain or snow, stationary temperature. No. 4. A black triangular flag placed above flag No. 1, indicates fair weather, warmer; placed below No. 1, indicates fair weather, colder; placed above No. 2, indicates rain or snow, warmer; placed below No. 2, indicates rain or snow, colder; placed above No. 3, indicates local rain or snow, warmer; placed below No. 3, indicates local rain or snow, colder. No. 5. A white flag with a black square in the centre indicates a cold wave. The signals described in this paragraph are not displayed at the Boston station.

Storm Signal. A red flag with a black centre indicates that a storm of marked violence is expected.

The pennants displayed with the flags indicate the direction of the wind; red, easterly (from northeast to south); white, westerly (from southwest to north). The pennant above the flag indicates that the wind is expected to blow from the northerly quadrants; below, from the southerly quadrants.

By night a red light indicates easterly winds, and a white light above a red light, westerly winds.

Information Signal. (Red or white pennant displayed alone.) When displayed at stations on the Great Lakes indicates that winds are expected which may prove dangerous to tows and smaller classes of vessels, the red pennant indicating easterly and the white pennant westerly winds.

When displayed at stations on the Atlantic, Pacific and Gulf coasts, indicates that the local observer has received information from the central office of a storm covering a limited area, dangerous only for vessels about to sail to certain points, and serves as a notification to shipmasters that information will be given them upon application to the local observer. Only the red pennant is displayed on the coasts.

Hurricane Signal. Two red flags with black centres, displayed one above the other, indicate the expected approach of tropical hurricanes, and also of those extremely severe and dangerous storms which occasionally move across the Lakes and northern Atlantic coast.

No night information or hurricane signals are displayed.

HOLIDAYS IN NEW ENGLAND.

The following days, *in respect to the payment of notes*, are legal holidays. On most of them courts, banks, etc., are closed. *If the day falls on Sunday, the day following is usually kept as a holiday. Thanksgiving and Fast are appointed by state or national authority.*

Maine. Jan. 1, Feb. 22, May 30, July 4, 1st Mo. Sept., Christmas, Fast and Thanksgiving. **New Hampshire.** Feb. 22, May 30, July 4, 1st Mon. Sept., Nov. 6 (Election Day), Christmas, Fast and Thanksgiving. **Vermont.** Jan. 1, Feb. 22, May 30, July 4, Aug. 16 (Bennington Battle Day), 1st Mon. Sept., Christmas and Thanksgiving. **Massachusetts.** Feb. 22, Apr. 19, May 30, July 4, 1st Mon. Sept., Christmas and Thanksgiving. **Rhode Island.** Jan. 1, Feb. 22, 2d Fri. May (Arbor Day), May 30, July 4, 1st Mon. Sept., Christmas, Thanksgiving and Election Days. **Connecticut.** Jan. 1, Feb. 12 (Lincoln Day) 22, May 30, July 4, 1st Mon. Sept., Christmas, Fast and Thanksgiving.

THE YEAR 1900 NOT A LEAP YEAR.

According to the Gregorian calendar, which is the one in use, all years whose number is divisible by four without a remainder, are leap years, unless they are century years. Century years are only leap years when their number is divisible by four hundred without a remainder. Consequently the year 1900 is not a leap year, but 1901 will be.

1900]   JANUARY, First Month.

ASTRONOMICAL CALCULATIONS.

⊙'s Declination.	Days.	d. m.	Days.	d. m.	Days.	d. m.	Days.	d. m.	Days.	d. m.	Days.	d. m.
	1	23s. 0	7	22 22	13	21 28	19	20 19	25	18 57		
	2	22 55	8	22 14	14	21 18	20	20 7	26	18 42		
	3	22 49	9	22 6	15	21 7	21	19 53	27	18 27		
	4	22 43	10	21 57	16	20 56	22	19 40	28	18 11		
	5	22 37	11	21 48	17	20 44	23	19 26	29	17 55		
	6	22 30	12	21 38	18	20 32	24	19 12	30	17 38		

● New Moon, 1st day, 8h. 52m., morning, E.
☽ First Quarter, 8th day, 0h. 40m., morning, W.
○ Full Moon, 15th day, 2h. 8m., evening, E.
☾ Last Quarter, 23d day, 6h. 53m., evening, E.
● New Moon, 30th day, 8h. 23m., evening, W.

Day of Year.	Day of Month.	Day of the Week.	⊙ Rises. h. m.	⊙ Sets. h. m.	Length of Days. h. m.	Day's Incr. h. m.	Sun Fast m.	Moon's Age.	Full Sea, Boston. Morn h.	Full Sea, Boston. Even h.	☽'s Place	☽ Sets. h. m.	☽ Souths. h. m.
1	1	M.	7 14	4 23	9 9	0 5	12	●	10¾	11¼	kn.	sets	11 54
2	2	Tu.	7 14	4 24	9 10	0 6	11	1	11¾	—	legs	6 2	0 53
3	3	W.	7 14	4 24	9 10	0 6	11	2	0¼	0½	legs	7 18	1 50
4	4	Th.	7 14	4 25	9 11	0 7	11	3	1	1¼	feet	8 34	2 44
5	5	Fr.	7 14	4 26	9 12	0 8	10	4	1¾	2¼	feet	9 48	3 36
6	6	Sa.	7 14	4 27	9 13	0 9	10	5	2¾	3	h'd	11 1	4 27
7	7	S.	7 14	4 28	9 14	0 10	9	6	3¾	4	h'd	morn	5 17
8	8	M.	7 14	4 29	9 15	0 11	9	7	4½	5	h'd	0 12	6 8
9	9	Tu.	7 14	4 30	9 16	0 12	8	8	5½	6	n'k	1 22	7 0
10	10	W.	7 13	4 31	9 18	0 14	8	9	6½	7	n'k	2 30	7 53
11	11	Th.	7 13	4 32	9 19	0 15	8	10	7½	8¼	arm	3 35	8 47
12	12	Fr.	7 13	4 33	9 20	0 16	7	11	8½	9¼	arm	4 34	9 40
13	13	Sa.	7 12	4 34	9 22	0 18	7	12	9½	10	br.	5 27	10 32
14	14	S.	7 12	4 36	9 24	0 20	6	13	10¼	10¾	br.	6 12	11 23
15	15	M.	7 11	4 37	9 26	0 22	6	○	11	11½	br.	rises	morn
16	16	Tu.	7 11	4 38	9 27	0 23	6	15	11¾	—	h'rt	5 51	0 10
17	17	W.	7 11	4 39	9 28	0 24	5	16	0¼	0½	h'rt	6 51	0 55
18	18	Th.	7 10	4 40	9 30	0 26	5	17	1	1	bel.	7 50	1 38
19	19	Fr.	7 9	4 42	9 33	0 29	5	18	1½	1¾	bel.	8 49	2 20
20	20	Sa.	7 8	4 43	9 35	0 31	4	19	2¼	2½	bel.	9 48	3 0
21	21	S.	7 8	4 44	9 36	0 32	4	20	2¾	3	rei.	10 47	3 41
22	22	M.	7 7	4 45	9 38	0 34	4	21	3½	3¾	rei.	11 48	4 23
23	23	Tu.	7 7	4 47	9 40	0 36	4	22	4¼	4½	sec.	morn	5 7
24	24	W.	7 6	4 48	9 42	0 38	3	23	5	5¼	sec.	0 50	5 54
25	25	Th.	7 5	4 49	9 44	0 40	3	24	6	6¼	sec.	1 53	6 44
26	26	Fr.	7 4	4 50	9 46	0 42	3	25	6¾	7¼	thi.	2 56	7 38
27	27	Sa.	7 3	4 52	9 49	0 45	3	26	7¾	8¼	thi.	3 56	8 35
28	28	S.	7 2	4 53	9 51	0 47	3	27	8¾	9¼	kn.	4 52	9 34
29	29	M.	7 1	4 54	9 53	0 49	2	28	9½	10¼	kn.	5 41	10 34
30	30	Tu.	7 1	4 56	9 55	0 51	2	●	10½	11	legs	sets	11 33
31	31	W.	7 0	4 57	9 57	0 53	2	1	11¼	11¾	legs	6 9	0 30

JANUARY hath 31 days. [1900

Yes, we will love thee, month of death,
Yes, we will call thee glad New Year,
Freeze with thy kiss my weary breath,
See, I am thine, I know no fear.—MRS. JANE G. AUSTIN.

D. M.	D. W.	Aspects, Holidays, Weather, Events, etc.	Farmer's Calendar.
1	M.	Circumcision. ☌ ♂ ☾. *Clear*	May the homes of the readers of the Farmer's Calendar during the year 1900, be surrounded and filled with whatever may be necessary to secure success in every good work. May the members of each home strive to wear a smiling countenance, speak only kind words, and do as many kind acts as possible; and thus make home so attractive that it will always be returned to with the highest pleasure. The farmer's as well as the mechanic's home, is made more attractive by having a few pot plants in the sitting room during the winter months. Geraniums are hardy and easily cared for, and, what is important, will blossom at all seasons of the year; some hardy pinks are desirable; a small orange tree with its ripening fruit is always interesting; and a few pots of strawberries are very attractive. The green leaves, the white blossoms and the ripening fruit in midwinter, afford an attraction not only to the members of the home, but to all visitors. Winter apples should be kept in a temperature about eight degrees above that which will freeze water; and they should not be disturbed until wanted for the market, or for use. The old practice of picking over apples every week to get the partially decayed to use in the family, was a very bad one, and has been abandoned by modern farmers as very wasteful.
2	Tu.	⊕ in Perih., ♀ g. h. lat. S.	
3	W.	☾ in Perig. ☌ ♀ ☾. *and*	
4	Th.	High tides. {1st. Mil. occu. of Cuba by U.S., 1899.	
5	Fr.	3d. Mass. legislature meets. *cold.* 6th. Franklin b.. Boston, 1706.	
6	Sa.	Epiphany. {1st. M. A. Mayhew, Boston publisher, d. 1899, aged 65.	
7	**G**	**1st Sunday aft. Epiphany.**	
8	M.	7th. ☌ ♀ ♄.	
9	Tu.	☿ in ♉. *Grows*	
10	W.	Medium tides. *warmer.*	
11	Th.	{13th. Nelson Dingley, M. C. from Me., d. 1899, aged 67.	
12	Fr.	☾ runs high.	
13	Sa.	☌ ♆ ☾.	
14	**G**	**2d Sunday aft. Epiphany.**	
15	M.		
16	Tu.	☌ ♂ ☉. *A*	
17	W.	{17th. J. Russell Young, Libr.-Cong., d. 1899, aged 57.	
18	Th.	Medium tides. *snow*	
19	Fr.	☾ in Apog., ☿ in Aphel.	
20	Sa.	*storm*	
21	**G**	**3d Sunday aft. Epiphany.**	
22	M.	*coming.*	
23	Tu.	{26th. Augustus H. Garland, ex-Attorney General U. S., d. 1899. aged 66.	
24	W.		
25	Th.	Conv. of St. Paul. Low tides.	
26	Fr.	☌ ♃ ☾, ☌ ♅ ☾.	
27	Sa.	☾ runs low.	
28	**G**	**4th Sunday aft. Epiphany.**	
29	M.	28th. ☌ ♄ ☾. *Cold*	
30	Tu.	☌ ☿ ☾, ☌ ♂ ☾. *weather.*	
31	W.	☾ in Perigee.	

1900] FEBRUARY, SECOND MONTH.

ASTRONOMICAL CALCULATIONS.

☉'s Declination.

Days.	d. m.	Days	d. m.	Days.	d. m.	Days.	d. m.	Days.	d. m.
1	17s. 4	7	15 17	13	13 20	19	11 15	25	9 4
2	16 48	8	14 58	14	13 0	20	10 54	26	8 42
3	16 30	9	14 39	15	12 39	21	10 32	27	8 19
4	16 12	10	14 20	16	12 19	22	10 10	28	7 56
5	15 54	11	14 0	17	11 58	23	9 48		
6	15 36	12	13 40	18	11 37	24	9 26		

☽ First Quarter, 6th day, 11h. 23m., morning, E.

○ Full Moon, 14th day, 8h. 50m., morning, W.

☾ Last Quarter, 22d day, 11h. 44m., morning, W.

Day of Year.	Day of Month.	Day of the Week.	☉ Rises. h. m.	☉ Sets. h. m.	Length of Days. h. m.	Day's Incr. h. m.	Sun Fast m.	Moon's Age.	Full Sea, Boston, Morn h.	Full Sea, Boston, Even h.	☽'s Place	☽ Sets. h. m.	☽ Souths. h. m.
32	1	Th.	6 58	4 58	10 0	0 56	2	2	--	0¼	feet	7 26	1 24
33	2	Fr.	6 57	5 0	10 3	0 59	2	3	0¾	1	feet	8 43	2 18
34	3	Sa.	6 56	5 1	10 5	1 1	2	4	1½	2	h'd	9 57	3 10
35	4	S.	6 55	5 2	10 7	1 3	2	5	2¼	2¾	h'd	11 10	4 3
36	5	M.	6 54	5 4	10 10	1 6	1	6	3¼	3¾	n'k	morn	4 56
37	6	Tu.	6 53	5 5	10 12	1 8	1	7	4¼	4¾	n'k	0 21	5 49
38	7	W.	6 52	5 6	10 14	1 10	1	8	5	5¾	arm	1 27	6 43
39	8	Th.	6 51	5 7	10 16	1 12	1	9	6	6¾	arm	2 28	7 37
40	9	Fr.	6 50	5 9	10 19	1 15	1	10	7¼	7¾	br.	3 23	8 29
41	10	Sa.	6 48	5 10	10 22	1 18	1	11	8	8¾	br.	4 10	9 19
42	11	S.	6 47	5 11	10 24	1 20	1	12	9	9¾	br.	4 50	10 7
43	12	M.	6 45	5 12	10 27	1 23	1	13	9¾	10½	h'rt	5 25	10 53
44	13	Tu.	6 44	5 14	10 30	1 26	1	14	10¾	11¼	h'rt	5 55	11 36
45	14	W.	6 43	5 15	10 32	1 28	1	○	11¼	11¾	bel.	rises	morn
46	15	Th.	6 42	5 16	10 34	1 30	1	16	—	0	bel.	6 41	0 18
47	16	Fr.	6 41	5 18	10 37	1 33	1	17	0½	0½	bel.	7 40	0 59
48	17	Sa.	6 39	5 19	10 40	1 36	1	18	1	1¼	rei.	8 38	1 40
49	18	S.	6 37	5 20	10 43	1 39	2	19	1½	1¾	rei.	9 38	2 21
50	19	M.	6 36	5 22	10 46	1 42	2	20	2¼	2½	sec.	10 39	3 4
51	20	Tu.	6 34	5 23	10 49	1 45	2	21	2¾	3¼	sec.	11 40	3 49
52	21	W.	6 33	5 24	10 51	1 47	2	22	3½	4	sec.	morn	4 37
53	22	Th.	6 32	5 25	10 53	1 49	2	23	4½	4¾	thi.	0 42	5 28
54	23	Fr.	6 30	5 26	10 56	1 52	2	24	5¼	5¾	thi.	1 42	6 22
55	24	Sa.	6 29	5 28	10 59	1 55	2	25	6¼	6¾	kn.	2 37	7 18
56	25	S.	6 27	5 29	11 2	1 58	2	26	7¼	7¾	kn.	3 28	8 16
57	26	M.	6 25	5 30	11 5	2 1	3	27	8¼	8¾	legs	4 13	9 13
58	27	Tu.	6 24	5 32	11 8	2 4	3	28	9¼	9¾	legs	4 52	10 10
59	28	W.	6 22	5 33	11 11	2 7	3	29	10¼	10¾	feet	5 28	11 6

MERCURY.

The most favorable times for seeing Mercury in 1900 will be about Mar. 8, July 4, and Oct. 29, in the west after sunset; and Apr. 21, Aug. 19, and Dec. 7, in the east before sunrise.

FEBRUARY hath 28 days. [1900

> But Winter has yet brighter scenes — he boasts
> Splendors beyond what gorgeous Summer knows;
> Or Autumn with his many fruits, and woods
> All flushed with many hues. — BYRANT.

D. M.	D. W.	Aspects, Holidays, Weather, Events, Etc.	Farmer's Calendar.
1	Th.	High tides.	The farmer should improve every opportunity this month to sled his logs to mill, or he may have to load them on wheels which very much increases the labor of loading. Moreover there are many wood-lots with roads to them too rough for wheels.
2	Fr.	Purifica. of V. Mary. Candlemas-Day.	
3	Sa.	☌ ☿ ♂. 2ᵈ. ☌ ♀ ☾. *Fine.*	
4	G	5th Sunday aft. Epiphany.	
5	M.	1st. Col. G. A. Saxton, G. A. R. com., d. 1899 aged 55.	
6	Tu.	6th. Count Caprivi, Ger. statesman, d. 1899, aged 68.	
7	W.	7th. John Williams, Bp. of Conn., d. 1899, ag. 81. *Warmer.*	Cattle require more care this month than in any other month in the year, especially the cows that come in early. They should not be kept out in the cold wind, or required to drink ice-water; yet they should be given a chance to get some exercise in sheltered yards during pleasant weather, and in dry sheds in stormy weather. To feed cattle to the best advantage requires the exercise of intelligence only acquired by practice and good judgment.
8	Th.	☾ runs high. ☿ gr. h. l. S.	
9	Fr.	Lo. ti. ☌ ♆ ☾, ☌ ☿ ⊙ sup.	
10	Sa.	10th. President signed peace treaty, 1899. 11th. Iloilo captured, 1899.	
11	G	Septuagesima Sunday. *A*	
12	M.	LINCOLN DAY, CONN. *N. E.*	
13	Tu.	13th. Severe snow storm, 1899.	
14	W.	St. Valentine. *storm*	
15	Th.	☾ in Apogee. *of*	
16	Fr.	Medium tides. *snow*	The long winter evenings should be utilized by those who have children, by giving such entertainments as are adapted to the ages of the children, and of a character which will tend to make them wiser and better, as well as happier and more closely attached to their homes. When farmers' sons find their homes less attractive than the corner grocery or the neighboring saloon, it would be well to find out why this is so; and advisable for farmers to endeavor to brighten up their homes, and
17	Sa.	16th. Pres. Faure, of France, d. 1899, aged 58. *or*	
18	G	Sexagesima Sunday.	
19	M.	18th. Emile Loubet elected French president, 1899. *rain.*	
20	Tu.	22d. WASHINGTON born, 1732.	
21	W.	24th. E. Welti, ex-Pres. of Switzer., d. 1899, aged 74.	
22	Th.	♂ gr. hel. lat. S., ☌ ♃ ☾.	
23	Fr.	☌ ☿ ☾, ☾ runs low.	
24	Sa.	St. Matthias. L. tides, ☌ ♄ ☾.	
25	G	Shrove Sunday. *Fine*	
26	M.	27th. Longfellow born, 1807. *again.*	
27	Tu.	☿ in ☟, ♀ in ☟.	
28	W.	Ash Wednes. ☐ ♃ ⊙, ☌ ♂ ☾.	

if possible make them so attractive that the boys will have no desire to leave them.

Give the sheep not only dry quarters, but also give them plenty of sun and pure air.

1900]

MARCH, Third Month.

ASTRONOMICAL CALCULATIONS.

☉'s Declination. Days.	d. m.	Days.	d. m.	Days.	d. m.	Days.	d. m.	Days.	d. m.
1	7s.34	7	5 15	13	2 54	19	0 32	25	1 50
2	7 11	8	4 52	14	2 31	20	0s. 8	26	2 13
3	6 48	9	4 28	15	2 7	21	0n.15	27	2 37
4	6 25	10	4 5	16	1 43	22	0 39	28	3 0
5	6 2	11	3 41	17	1 20	23	1 3	29	3 24
6	5 38	12	3 18	18	0 56	24	1 26	30	3 47

● New Moon, 1st day, 6h. 25m., morning, E.
☽ First Quarter, 8th day, 0h. 34m., morning, W.
○ Full Moon, 16th day, 3h. 12m., morning, W.
☾ Last Quarter, 24th day, 0h. 36m., morning, E.
● New Moon, 30th day, 3h. 30m., evening, W.

Day of Year.	Day of Month.	Day of the Week.	☉ Rises. h. m.	☉ Sets. h. m.	Length of Days. h. m.	Day's Incr. h. m.	Sun Fast m.	Moon's Age.	Full Sea, Boston. Morn h.	Full Sea, Boston. Even h.	☽'s Place	☽ Sets. h. m.	☽ Souths. h. m.
60	1	Th.	6 20	5 34	11 14	2 10	3	●	11	11½	feet	sets	0 1
61	2	Fr.	6 19	5 35	11 16	2 12	3	1	11¾	—	h'd	7 32	0 56
62	3	Sa.	6 17	5 36	11 19	2 15	4	2	0¼	0¾	h'd	8 48	1 50
63	4	S.	6 16	5 38	11 22	2 18	4	3	1¼	1½	n'k	10 3	2 45
64	5	M.	6 14	5 39	11 25	2 21	4	4	2	2½	n'k	11 14	3 41
65	6	Tu.	6 12	5 40	11 28	2 24	4	5	2¾	3¼	arm	morn	4 36
66	7	W.	6 11	5 41	11 30	2 26	4	6	3¾	4¼	arm	0 19	5 31
67	8	Th.	6 9	5 42	11 33	2 29	5	7	4¾	5¼	arm	1 18	6 25
68	9	Fr.	6 7	5 43	11 36	2 32	5	8	5¾	6½	br.	2 8	7 16
69	10	Sa.	6 6	5 45	11 39	2 35	5	9	6¾	7½	br.	2 50	8 5
70	11	S.	6 4	5 46	11 42	2 38	6	10	7¾	8½	h'rt	3 27	8 51
71	12	M.	6 2	5 47	11 45	2 41	6	11	8¾	9¼	h'rt	3 58	9 35
72	13	Tu.	6 0	5 48	11 48	2 44	6	12	9½	10	hr't	4 25	10 17
73	14	W.	5 59	5 49	11 50	2 46	6	13	10¼	10¾	bel.	4 50	10 58
74	15	Th.	5 57	5 50	11 53	2 49	7	14	11	11¼	bel.	5 14	11 39
75	16	Fr.	5 56	5 52	11 56	2 52	7	○	11½	11¾	rei.	rises	morn
76	17	Sa.	5 54	5 53	11 59	2 55	7	16	—	0¼	rei.	7 31	0 20
77	18	S.	5 52	5 54	12 2	2 58	7	17	0½	0¾	rei.	8 32	1 3
78	19	M.	5 50	5 55	12 5	3 1	8	18	1	1½	sec.	9 33	1 47
79	20	Tu.	5 48	5 56	12 8	3 4	8	19	1¾	2	sec.	10 34	2 34
80	21	W.	5 46	5 57	12 11	3 7	8	20	2¼	2¾	thi.	11 33	3 23
81	22	Th.	5 44	5 58	12 14	3 10	9	21	3	3½	thi.	morn	4 15
82	23	Fr.	5 43	6 0	12 17	3 13	9	22	4	4½	kn.	0 29	5 9
83	24	Sa.	5 41	6 1	12 20	3 16	9	23	4¾	5½	kn.	1 20	6 5
84	25	S.	5 40	6 2	12 22	3 18	10	24	5¾	6½	kn.	2 6	7 0
85	26	M.	5 38	6 3	12 25	3 21	10	25	7	7½	legs	2 46	7 56
86	27	Tu.	5 36	6 4	12 28	3 24	10	26	8	8½	legs	3 22	8 50
87	28	W.	5 34	6 5	12 31	3 27	11	27	8¾	9¼	feet	3 55	9 44
88	29	Th.	5 32	6 6	12 34	3 30	11	28	9¾	10¼	feet	4 27	10 38
89	30	Fr.	5 31	6 8	12 37	3 33	11	●	10¾	11	h'd	sets	11 33
90	31	Sa.	5 29	6 9	12 40	3 36	11	1	11½	—	h'd	7 36	0 28

MARCH hath 31 days. [1900

Come now, like Pan's old crew, we'll dance and sing:
Or Oberon's; for hill and valley ring
To March's bugle-horn, — Earth's blood is stirred.

WM. ALLINGHAM.

D. M.	D. W.	Aspects, Holidays, Events, Weather, Etc.	Farmer's Calendar.
1	Th.	St. David. ☾ in Perigee. *Cold*	During this month the intelligent farmer will decide what crops he intends to grow the coming season, and if seed is to be bought, he will buy in season to test its germinating qualities. This is important if success is to be assured.
2	Fr.	High tides, ☌ ☿ ☾.	
3	Sa.	□ ♅ ☉. 4th. ☿ in Perih.	
4	**C**	1st Sun. in Lent. ☌ ♀ ☾.	
5	M.	♆ stat. *and*	
6	Tu.	4th. Mass. charter granted, 1629. 5th. Boston Massacre, 1770.	
7	W.	{6th. Princess Kaiulani, of Hawaii, { d. 1899. aged 23.	The stormy days of this month furnish a good opportunity to examine the farm implements, and if any are not in good order, to make such repairs as may be necessary to fit them to do good work. It is a very wasteful practice to put off the repairs of a machine until it is wanted, and then rush to some repair shop only to find the mechanic so full of business that he cannot do the repairing for several days. In the meantime the season advances, and the planting is too late for a good crop because of the neglect to repair the farm implements at the proper time.
8	Th.	☾ runs high, ☿ gr. el. E.	
9	Fr.	8th. ☌ ♆ ☾. *uncom-*	
10	Sa.	Low tides. *fortable.*	
11	**C**	2d Sunday in Lent.	
12	M.	*Becomes*	
13	Tu.	14th. ☿ stationary.	
14	W.	☾ in Apog., ☿ g. h. lat. N.	
15	Th.	□ ♆ ☉. {14th. E. Erckmann, French { novelist, d. 1899, aged 76.	
16	Fr.	{16th. Spain ratified peace *warmer.* { treaty, 1899.	
17	Sa.	St. Patrick. ♅ stationary.	
18	**C**	3d Su. iu L. Med. tides.	
19	M.	18th. ♂ in Perih. *Rain*	
20	Tu.	☉ enters ♈. SPRING BEGINS.	
21	W.	St. Benedict. *or snow.*	Do not forget to set a few hens to keep up the stock of laying hens next autumn, when eggs will bring a good price.
22	Th.	☽ r. low, ☌ ♃ ☾, ☌ ♅ ☾.	
23	Fr.	26th. Battle of Caloocan, 1899.	
24	Sa.	L. tide. ☌ ♄ ☾, ☌ ☿ ☉ inf.	If you wish to make a good show of Chrysanthemums next November, the cuttings should have been set the last of February or the first of this month. All early flowering bulbs should be uncovered as soon as the snow is gone.
25	**C**	4th. S. in Lent. An. or Lady Day.	
26	M.	25th. □ ♄ ☉.	
27	Tu.	♃ stat. {28th. Birket Foster, English { artist, d. 1899. aged 74.	
28	W.	{29th. Gen. D. W. Flagler, U. S. A. { d. 1899. aged 64.	
29	Th.	☾ in Perigee, ☌ ♂ ☾.	Put the walks around the dwelling in good condition as soon as the frost is well out of the ground.
30	Fr.	☌ ☿ ☾.	
31	Sa.	31st. Malolos occupied, 1899. 31st. Bost. Port Bill passed, 1774. *Fair.*	

1900] APRIL, Fourth Month.

ASTRONOMICAL CALCULATIONS.

	Days.	d. m.	Days.	d. m.	Days.	d. m.	Days.	d. m.	Days.	d. m.	Days.	d. m.
⊙'s Declination.	1	4N.34	7	6 51	13	9 4	19	11 11	25	13 12		
	2	4 57	8	7 13	14	9 25	20	11 32	26	13 32		
	3	5 20	9	7 36	15	9 47	21	11 52	27	13 51		
	4	5 43	10	7 58	16	10 8	22	12 13	28	14 10		
	5	6 5	11	8 20	17	10 29	23	12 33	29	14 29		
	6	6 28	12	8 42	18	10 50	24	12 52	30	14 47		

☽ First Quarter, 6th day, 3h. 55m., evening, E.

○ Full Moon, 14th day, 8h. 2m., evening, E.

☾ Last Quarter, 22d day, 9h. 33m., morning, W.

● New Moon, 29th day, 0h. 23m., morning E.

Day of Year.	Day of Month.	Day of the Week.	⊙ Rises. h. m.	Sets. h. m.	Length of Days. h. m.	Day's Incr. h. m.	Sun Fast	Moon's Age.	Full Sea, Boston. Morn h.	Even h.	☽'s Place	☽ Sets. h. m.	☽ Souths. h. m.
91	1	S.	5 27	6 10	12 43	3 39	12	2	0	0½	n'k	8 51	1 25
92	2	M.	5 26	6 11	12 45	3 41	12	3	0¾	1¼	n'k	10 1	2 22
93	3	Tu.	5 24	6 12	12 48	3 44	12	4	1½	2	arm	11 5	3 20
94	4	W.	5 22	6 13	12 51	3 47	13	5	2½	3	arm	11 59	4 16
95	5	Th.	5 20	6 14	12 54	3 50	13	6	3¼	4	br.	morn	5 9
96	6	Fr.	5 19	6 16	12 57	3 53	13	7	4¼	4¾	br.	0 47	6 0
97	7	Sa.	5 17	6 17	13 0	3 56	13	8	5¼	6	h'rt	1 25	6 47
98	8	S.	5 15	6 18	13 3	3 59	14	9	6¼	7	h'rt	1 59	7 32
99	9	M.	5 14	6 19	13 5	4 1	14	10	7¼	7¾	h'rt	2 28	8 15
100	10	Tu.	5 12	6 20	13 8	4 4	14	11	8	8¾	bel.	2 53	8 56
101	11	W.	5 10	6 21	13 11	4 7	15	12	9	9½	bel.	3 18	9 37
102	12	Th.	5 9	6 22	13 13	4 9	15	13	9¾	10	bel.	3 42	10 19
103	13	Fr.	5 7	6 23	13 16	4 12	15	14	10¼	10¾	rei.	4 6	11 1
104	14	Sa.	5 5	6 24	13 19	4 15	15	○ 11	11¼	rei.	rises	11 45
105	15	S.	5 4	6 26	13 22	4 18	16	16	11¾	—	sec.	7 25	morn
106	16	M.	5 2	6 27	13 25	4 21	16	17	0	0¼	sec.	8 27	0 32
107	17	Tu.	5 1	6 28	13 27	4 23	16	18	0½	1	thi.	9 27	1 21
108	18	W.	4 59	6 29	13 30	4 26	16	19	1¼	1¾	thi.	10 24	2 12
109	19	Th.	4 58	6 30	13 32	4 28	17	20	2	2½	thi.	11 16	3 5
110	20	Fr.	4 56	6 31	13 35	4 31	17	21	2¾	3¼	kn.	morn	4 0
111	21	Sa.	4 54	6 32	13 38	4 34	17	22	3½	4¼	kn.	0 3	4 54
112	22	S.	4 53	6 33	13 40	4 36	17	23	4½	5	legs	0 44	5 48
113	23	M.	4 51	6 34	13 43	4 39	17	24	5½	6	legs	1 20	6 41
114	24	Tu.	4 50	6 36	13 46	4 42	18	25	6½	7	feet	1 53	7 34
115	25	W.	4 48	6 37	13 49	4 45	18	26	7½	8	feet	2 24	8 25
116	26	Th.	4 47	6 38	13 51	4 47	18	27	8½	9	h'd	2 55	9 18
117	27	Fr.	4 46	6 39	13 53	4 49	18	28	9½	9¾	h'd	3 26	10 12
118	28	Sa.	4 44	6 40	13 56	4 52	18	29	10¼	10¾	n'k	4 1	11 7
119	29	S.	4 43	6 41	13 58	4 54	18	●	11¼	11½	n'k	sets	0 5
120	30	M.	4 41	6 42	14 1	4 57	19	1	—	0	arm	8 45	1 3

APRIL hath 30 days. [1900

April, April,
Laugh thy golden laughter,
But, the moment after,
Weep thy golden tears. — WM. WATSON.

D. M.	D. W.	Aspects, Holidays, Events, Weather, Etc.	Farmer's Calendar.
1	G	5th Su. in L. High tides.	The New England farmer will always find plenty of work this month. If his wood was cut and prepared for the stove when it should have been, it will now be in good condition to house.
2	M.	♀ in Perihel., ☌ ♀ ☾.	
3	Tu.	☌ ☿ ☌ . {1st. Naval officers killed in Samoa, 1899.	
4	W.	☾ runs high, ☌ ♆ ☾.	
5	Th.	4th. Election in Rhode Island. 9th. Judge Stephen J. Field d. '99, ag. 82.	The fences on the farm should be looked after, and new ones set where the old ones are too much out of order to repair. Never delay this work until pasturing time comes, and then be compelled to leave the planting and other important work, that the cattle may be turned out to pasture.
6	Fr.	☿ stat. Variable	
7	Sa.	☿ in ☍. {11th. Peace with Spain ratified, 1899.	
8	G	Palm Sunday. Low tides.	
9	M.	{17th. Eli Thayer, ex-M. C. f'm Mass., d. 1899, ag. 80. weather.	
10	Tu.	17th. Minot's lighthouse destroyed, 1851. 18th. Gov. Andros deposed, 1689.	
11	W.	☾ in Apogee. Expect	
12	Th.	{21st. John T. Wait, ex-M. C. from Conn., d. 1899, aged 88. a	During this month the mowing fields should be looked over and everything that will obstruct the mower removed ; thus saving work in grinding knives, or injury to the machine.
13	Fr.	Good Friday. storm.	
14	Sa.	♄ stationary.	
15	G	Easter Sunday.	
16	M.	{24th. Ex-Gov. R. J. Oglesby, Ill., d. 1899, ag. 75.	Set a few fruit trees in the orchard, and do not neglect to set a few strawberry vines in the garden. Always set currant bushes where the plough and cultivator can be run on both sides of the row, and not on one side of the garden where it will be difficult to keep the grass out. Do not neglect to set a few ornamental trees and flowering shrubs around your dwelling; but never set trees, that grow to a large size, so near the house as to shut out all of the sunshine.
17	Tu.	☿ in Aph. Warmer.	
18	W.	Med. tid. ☿ ♃ ☾, ☌ ⚥ ☾.	
19	Th.	PATRIOTS' DAY. ☾ runs low.	
20	Fr.	☌ ♄ ☾. Pleasant	
21	Sa.	☿ gr. elong. W.	
22	G	Low Sunday.	
23	M.	St. George. with	
24	Tu.	♀ gr. hel. lat. N.	
25	W.	St. Mark. 25th. Cromwell born, 1599.	
26	Th.	☾ in Perigee. showers.	
27	Fr.	☌ ☿ ☾, ☌ ☌ ☾.	Whatever you do for your home, see that it does not shut out the sunshine of happiness, or a glimmer of light which will gladden the hearts of a single member.
28	Sa.	♀ gr. elong. E.	
29	G	2d Su. aft. E. H. tides.	
30	M.	☌ ♀ ♆. 27th. U. S. Grant b. 1822.	

1900]

MAY, FIFTH MONTH.

ASTRONOMICAL CALCULATIONS.

☉'s Declination.

Days.	d. m.	Days.	d. m.	Days.	d. m.	Days.	d. m.	Days.	d. m.
1	15N.5	7	16 49	13	18 24	19	19 47	25	20 58
2	15 23	8	17 6	14	18 38	20	19 59	26	21 8
3	15 41	9	17 22	15	18 53	21	20 12	27	21 18
4	15 59	10	17 38	16	19 7	22	20 24	28	21 28
5	16 16	11	17 53	17	19 20	23	20 35	29	21 38
6	16 33	12	18 9	18	19 34	24	20 47	30	21 47

☽ First Quarter, 6th day, 8h. 39m., morning, E.
○ Full Moon, 14th day, 10h. 37m., morning, W.
☾ Last Quarter, 21st day, 3h. 31m., evening, W.
● New Moon, 28th day, 9h. 50m., morning, E.

Day of Year.	Day of Month.	Day of the Week.	☉ Rises. h. m.	☉ Sets. h. m.	Length of Days. h. m.	Day's Incr. h. m.	Sun Fast m.	Moon's Age.	Full Sea, Boston. Morn h.	Full Sea, Boston. Even h.	☽'s Place	☽ Sets. h. m.	☽ Souths. h. m.
121	1	Tu.	4 40	6 43	14 3	4 59	19	2	0¼	1	arm	9 46	2 1
122	2	W.	4 38	6 44	14 6	5 2	19	3	1¼	1¾	br.	10 38	2 57
123	3	Th.	4 37	6 46	14 9	5 5	19	4	2	2½	br.	11 22	3 50
124	4	Fr.	4 36	6 47	14 11	5 7	19	5	3	3½	br.	11 57	4 40
125	5	Sa.	4 35	6 48	14 13	5 9	19	6	3¾	4½	h'rt	morn	5 27
126	6	S.	4 33	6 49	14 16	5 12	19	7	4¾	5¼	h'rt	0 28	6 11
127	7	M.	4 32	6 50	14 18	5 14	19	8	5½	6¼	bel.	0 56	6 53
128	8	Tu.	4 31	6 51	14 20	5 16	19	9	6½	7¼	bel.	1 20	7 34
129	9	W.	4 30	6 52	14 22	5 18	19	10	7½	8	bel.	1 44	8 15
130	10	Th.	4 29	6 53	14 24	5 20	19	11	8¼	8¾	rei.	2 9	8 57
131	11	Fr.	4 27	6 54	14 27	5 23	19	12	9	9¼	rei.	2 34	9 41
132	12	Sa.	4 26	6 55	14 29	5 25	19	13	9¾	10	sec.	3 2	10 27
133	13	S.	4 25	6 56	14 31	5 27	20	14	10½	10¾	sec.	3 33	11 15
134	14	M.	4 24	6 57	14 33	5 29	20	○	11¼	11¼	sec.	**rises**	morn
135	15	Tu.	4 23	6 58	14 35	5 31	20	16	11¾	—	thi.	8 18	0 7
136	16	W.	4 22	6 59	14 37	5 33	20	17	0	0½	thi.	9 13	1 0
137	17	Th.	4 21	7 0	14 39	5 35	19	18	0¾	1¼	kn.	10 2	1 55
138	18	Fr.	4 20	7 1	14 41	5 37	19	19	1½	2	kn.	10 44	2 51
139	19	Sa.	4 19	7 2	14 43	5 39	19	20	2½	3	legs	11 22	3 45
140	20	S.	4 18	7 3	14 45	5 41	19	21	3¼	3¾	legs	11 55	4 38
141	21	M.	4 18	7 4	14 46	5 42	19	22	4¼	4¾	feet	morn	5 29
142	22	Tu.	4 17	7 5	14 48	5 44	19	23	5¼	5¾	feet	0 27	6 20
143	23	W.	4 16	7 6	14 50	5 46	19	24	6¼	6¾	h'd	0 56	7 11
144	24	Th.	4 15	7 7	14 52	5 48	19	25	7¼	7¾	h'd	1 26	8 2
145	25	Fr.	4 14	7 8	14 54	5 50	19	26	8¼	8½	h'd	1 58	8 55
146	26	Sa.	4 14	7 9	14 55	5 51	19	27	9¼	9½	n'k	2 35	9 50
147	27	S.	4 13	7 10	14 57	5 53	19	28	10	10½	n'k	3 16	10 47
148	28	M.	4 12	7 11	14 59	5 55	19	●	11	11¼	arm	**sets**	11 45
149	29	Tu.	4 12	7 12	15 0	5 56	19	1	11¾	—	arm	8 26	0 43
150	30	W.	4 11	7 12	15 1	5 57	18	2	0	0¾	br.	9 14	1 38
151	31	Th.	4 10	7 13	15 3	5 59	18	3	0¾	1½	br.	9 54	2 30

MAY hath 31 days. [1900

While yet the year is young
Many a garland shall be hung
In our gardens of the dead;
On obelisk and urn
Shall the lilac's purple burn,
And the wild-rose leaves be shed.—T. B. ALDRICH.

D. M.	D. W.	Aspects, Holidays, Events, Weather, Etc.	Farmer's Calendar.
1	Tu.	St. Philip and St. James. H. tides.	The tent caterpillar, canker worm, asparagus beetle, currant worm, cut worm and the black spicy squash bug, rarely fail to put in an appearance during some portion of this month; and if the farmer is to get his share of the crops, he must be on hand with those compounds which he has so often been informed are effective for their destruction. The farmer no sooner gets master of the destructive insects, than there comes another plague called fungi, which, if not hindered or destroyed by frequently spraying the shrubs and trees, will greatly injure the leaves and the quality of the fruit in both the garden and orchard. The rapid increase of the enemies to both fruits and vegetables makes May, to the farmer the busiest month in the year. Never half plough land for either field or garden crops; but plough it well, and then thoroughly prepare the soil by making it fine and mixing the fertilizer with it as evenly and as thoroughly as possible. Plants will not grow well in a soil that is full of hard lumps of earth; the soil should be so well pulverized as to give the air a free circulation through it. Give the young chicks good yard room where they can have plenty of grass, or they will not grow well. Spring lambs should have a good pasture to run in; there is nothing better for them than white clover.
2	W.	☌♄☾, ☌♀☾. *Cool*	
3	Th.	☌☿☌. {1st. Boston became a city, 1822.	
4	Fr.	1st. ☾ runs high. *but*	
5	Sa.	{8th. Wm. Lawrence, ex-comp. U.S. Treas., d. 1899, aged 80.	
6	G	3d Sunday aft. Easter.	
7	M.	☿ gr. hel. lat. S. *pleasant*	
8	Tu.	Low tides. ☾ in Apogee.	
9	W.	{12th. Ex-Gov. R. P. Flower d. 1899, aged 63.	
10	Th.	14th. Second Mass. charter arrived, 1692.	
11	Fr.	ARBOR DAY, R. I. *and*	
12	Sa.	{15th. Francisque Sarcey, Fr. critic, d. 1899. aged 70.	
13	G	4th Sunday after Easter.	
14	M.	16th. ☾ runs low.	
15	Tu.	☌♃☾, ☌♅☾ *agreeable*	
16	W.	Med. tides. {20th. Adm. Dewey left Manila, 1899.	
17	Th.	☌♄☾. *weather.*	
18	Fr.	{20th. Wm. Ware, Boston publisher, d. 1899, aged 59.	
19	Sa.	24th. Queen Victoria born, 1819.	
20	G	Rogation Sunday. *Look*	
21	M.	{15th. E. Castelar, Span. statesman, d. 1899, aged 66.	
22	Tu.	{15th. Rosa Bonheur, French artist, d. 1899, aged 77.	
23	W.	29th. R.I. legislature meets. *out*	
24	Th.	Holy Thursday. ☾ in Perigee.	
25	Fr.	27th. High tides. *for*	
26	Sa.	☌☌☾, ☿ in ♌. *rain.*	
27	G	Sun. af. Ascension. ☍♃☉.	
28	M.	☉ partly ecl., vis. ☌☿☾.	
29	Tu.	☾ r. high. ☌♄☾. *Warmer.*	
30	W.	MEMORIAL DAY. ☌☿☉ sup.	
31	Th.	☿ in Perihelion, ☌♀☾.	

| 1900] | JUNE, Sixth Month. |

ASTRONOMICAL CALCULATIONS.

⊙'s Declination.	Days.	d. m.	Days.	d. m.	Days.	d. m.	Days.	d. m.	Days.	d. m.	Days.	d. m.
	1	22 N. 4	7	22 46	13	23 13	19	23 26	25	23 24
	2	22 12	8	22 51	14	23 16	20	23 27	26	23 22
	3	22 19	9	22 56	15	23 19	21	23 27	27	23 20
	4	22 27	10	23 1	16	23 22	22	23 27	28	23 17
	5	22 33	11	23 6	17	23 23	23	23 26	29	23 14
	6	22 40	12	23 10	18	23 25	24	23 25	30	23 11

☽ First Quarter, 5th day, 1h. 59m., morning, W.

○ Full Moon, 12th day, 10h. 38m., evening, E.

☾ Last Quarter, 19th day, 7h. 57m., evening, E.

● New Moon, 26th day, 8h. 27m., evening, W.

Day of Year.	Day of Month.	Day of the Week.	⊙ Rises. h. m.	⊙ Sets. h. m.	Length of Days. h. m.	Day's Incr. h. m.	Sun Fast. m.	Moon's Age.	Full Sea. Boston. Morn h.	Full Sea. Boston. Even h.	☽'s Place	☽ Sets. h. m.	☽ Souths. h. m.
152	1	Fr.	4 10	7 14	15 4	6 0	18	4	1¾	2¼	h'rt	10 28	3 19
153	2	Sa.	4 10	7 15	15 5	6 1	18	5	2½	3	h'rt	10 57	4 5
154	3	S.	4 9	7 15	15 6	6 2	18	6	3¼	4	h'rt	11 23	4 48
155	4	M.	4 9	7 16	15 7	6 3	18	7	4	4¾	bel.	11 47	5 30
156	5	Tu.	4 8	7 17	15 9	6 5	17	8	5	5½	bel.	morn	6 11
157	6	W.	4 8	7 18	15 10	6 6	17	9	5¾	6¼	rei.	0 11	6 52
158	7	Th.	4 8	7 19	15 11	6 7	17	10	6¾	7¼	rei.	0 35	7 35
159	8	Fr.	4 7	7 19	15 12	6 8	17	11	7½	8	rei.	1 2	8 20
160	9	Sa.	4 7	7 20	15 13	6 9	17	12	8¼	8¾	sec.	1 32	9 7
161	10	S.	4 7	7 20	15 13	6 9	17	13	9	9½	sec.	2 6	9 57
162	11	M.	4 7	7 21	15 14	6 10	16	14	10	10¼	thi.	2 46	10 51
163	12	Tu.	4 7	7 21	15 14	6 10	16	○	10¾	11	thi.	rises	11 46
164	13	W.	4 7	7 22	15 15	6 11	16	16	11½	11¾	kn.	7 56	morn
165	14	Th.	4 7	7 22	15 15	6 11	16	17	—	0¼	kn.	8 43	0 43
166	15	Fr.	4 7	7 23	15 16	6 12	16	18	0½	1	legs	9 23	1 39
167	16	Sa.	4 7	7 23	15 16	6 12	15	19	1¼	1¾	legs	9 57	2 34
168	17	S.	4 7	7 23	15 16	6 12	15	20	2	2¾	legs	10 30	3 26
169	18	M.	4 7	7 24	15 17	6 13	15	21	3	3½	feet	11 0	4 18
170	19	Tu.	4 7	7 24	15 17	6 13	15	22	3¾	4½	feet	11 30	5 8
171	20	W.	4 7	7 24	15 17	6 13	14	23	4¾	5¼	h'd	morn	5 59
172	21	Th.	4 7	7 24	15 17	Dec.	14	24	5¾	6¼	h'd	0 1	6 50
173	22	Fr.	4 7	7 24	15 17	0 0	14	25	6¾	7¼	n'k	0 34	7 43
174	23	Sa.	4 8	7 25	15 17	0 0	14	26	7¾	8¼	n'k	1 12	8 38
175	24	S.	4 8	7 25	15 17	0 0	14	27	8¾	9¼	arm	1 56	9 34
176	25	M.	4 9	7 25	15 16	0 1	13	28	9¾	10	arm	2 47	10 31
177	26	Tu.	4 9	7 25	15 16	0 1	13	●	10¾	11	br.	sets	11 27
178	27	W.	4 9	7 25	15 16	0 1	13	1	11½	11¾	br.	7 50	0 20
179	28	Th.	4 10	7 25	15 15	0 2	13	2	—	0¼	br.	8 26	1 11
180	29	Fr.	4 10	7 25	15 15	0 2	13	3	0½	1	h'rt	8 57	1 58
181	30	Sa.	4 10	7 25	15 15	0 2	12	4	1¼	1¾	h'rt	9 24	2 43

JUNE hath 30 days. [1900

In the blue of heaven holy
Clouds go floating, floating slowly,
Pure in snowy robe and sunny silver crown;
And they seem like gentle angels—
Leisure-full and loitering angels,
Looking down. — EDWARD R. SILL.

D. M.	D. W.	Aspects, Holidays, Events, Weather, Etc.	Farmer's Calendar.
1	Fr.	Nicomede. ♀ gr. bril., ☌ ♅ ☉.	Stir the soil frequently, not only to kill the weeds, but also to keep it in good condition. Until the crops shade the ground, cultivation is necessary to keep the surface of the soil from forming a hard crust after a heavy shower, which always checks the growth of annual plants. When plants get large enough to shade the whole surface of the land about them cultivation, as a rule, may cease, and no crust will form. Never cultivate the soil when it rains; but do so as soon after the rain ceases as the earth becomes dry enough to be easily pulverized. Never plant the home garden all at one time, but begin to plant peas in March, and plant a few every two weeks until the 15th of June. Begin to plant sweet corn the middle of April, and plant every two weeks until July. To have a succession of crops it is not necessary to plant early and late varieties, but plant the best varieties of peas, corn and beans. The first planting may not be quite as early as might be done with some very early variety, but the quality will be enough better to pay for waiting a few days longer. If you have only a small strawberry bed for home use, when the showers do not come often enough to keep the ground as wet as desired, water by hand labor, and thus secure a good crop even in a very dry season.
2	Sa.	{1st. Ancient and Honorable Artillery Company organized, 1638.	
3	G	Whit-Sunday. Fair	
4	M.	{3d. Joh. Strauss, Austrian composer, d. 1899, aged 74.	
5	Tu.	☾ in Apogee. warm and	
6	W.	{6th. Ex-mayor F. O. Prince, Boston, d. 1899, aged 81.	
7	Th.	Corpus Christi. L. tides. ☌ ☿ ♆.	
8	Fr.	{7th. Augustin Daly, manager, d. 1899, aged 61.	
9	Sa.	{10th. Henry Nichols, captain of Monadnock, d. 1899.	
10	G	Trinity Sun. ☿ gr. h. lat. N.	
11	M.	St. Barnabas. ☌ ♃ ☾. [ecl., vis.	
12	Tu.	☾ r. low, ☌ ♅ ☾, ☾ partly	
13	W.	Medium tides. ☌ ♄ ☾.	
14	Th.	14th. American flag adopted, 1777.	
15	Fr.	♀ stationary. Pleasant.	
16	Sa.	{15th. R. P. Bland, M. C. from Missouri, d. 1899, aged 64.	
17	G	1st Sun. aft. Trinity.	
18	M.	☾ in Perigee, High tides.	
19	Tu.	♀ in ♊. 18th. ☌ ♆ ☉.	
20	W.	17th. Battle of Bunker Hill, 1775. 17th. Louisburg captured, 1745.	
21	Th.	☉ enters ♋. {Summer begins.}	
22	Fr.	☌ ☿ ♀.	
23	Sa.	☌ ♄ ☉. 24th. ☌ ♂ ☾.	
24	G	2d Su. af. Trin. St. John, Bapt.	
25	M.	☾ runs high. High tides.	
26	Tu.	☌ ♆ ☾. Quite	
27	W.	{25th. Samuel Harris, Yale Theo. Sem., d. 1899, aged 85.	
28	Th.	☌ ♀ ☾. Tea taxed, 1767. warm.	
29	Fr.	St. Peter and St. Paul. ☌ ☿ ☾.	
30	Sa.	{30th. Mrs. E. D. E. N. Southworth, authoress, d. 1899, aged 80.	

1900] JULY, Seventh Month.

ASTRONOMICAL CALCULATIONS.

	Days.	d. m.	Days.	d. m.	Days.	d. m.	Days.	d. m.	Days.	d. m.
☉'s Declination.	1	23N.7	7	22 36	13	21 50	19	20 52	25	19 40
	2	23 3	8	22 29	14	21 42	20	20 41	26	19 27
	3	22 58	9	22 22	15	21 32	21	20 29	27	19 14
	4	22 53	10	22 15	16	21 23	22	20 17	28	19 0
	5	22 48	11	22 7	17	21 13	23	20 5	29	18 46
	6	22 42	12	21 59	18	21 2	24	19 53	30	18 31

☽ First Quarter, 4th day, 7h. 14m., evening, W.
○ Full Moon, 12th day, 8h. 22m., morning, W.
☾ Last Quarter, 19th day, 0h. 31m., morning, E.
● New Moon, 26th day, 8h. 43m., morning, E.

Day of Year.	Day of Month.	Day of the Week.	☉ Rises. h. m.	Sets. h. m.	Length of Days. h. m.	Day's Decr. h. m.	Sun Fast. m.	Moon's Age.	Full Sea, Boston. Morn h.	Even h.	☽'s Place	☽ Rises. h. m.	☽ Souths. h. m.
182	1	S.	4 11	7 25	15 14	0 3	12	5	2	2½	bel	9 49	3 25
183	2	M.	4 11	7 24	15 13	0 4	12	6	2¾	3¼	bel	10 14	4 7
184	3	Tu.	4 12	7 24	15 12	0 5	12	7	3½	4	rei.	10 38	4 48
185	4	W.	4 12	7 24	15 12	0 5	12	8	4¼	4¾	rei.	11 4	5 30
186	5	Th.	4 13	7 24	15 11	0 6	11	9	5	5½	rei.	11 31	6 13
187	6	Fr.	4 14	7 24	15 10	0 7	11	10	5¾	6¼	sec.	morn	6 58
188	7	Sa.	4 14	7 23	15 9	0 8	11	11	6¾	7¼	sec.	0 3	7 47
189	8	S.	4 15	7 23	15 8	0 9	11	12	7¾	8	thi.	0 40	8 39
190	9	M.	4 16	7 23	15 7	0 10	11	13	8½	8¾	thi.	1 24	9 33
191	10	Tu.	4 16	7 22	15 6	0 11	11	14	9¼	9¾	thi.	2 16	10 30
192	11	W.	4 17	7 22	15 5	0 12	10	15	10¼	10½	kn.	3 16	11 27
193	12	Th.	4 18	7 21	15 3	0 14	10	○	11	11¼	kn.	**rises**	morn
194	13	Fr.	4 19	7 21	15 2	0 15	10	17	11¾	—	legs	7 57	0 24
195	14	Sa.	4 19	7 20	15 1	0 16	10	18	0	0½	legs	8 31	1 19
196	15	S.	4 20	7 20	15 0	0 17	10	19	1	1½	feet	9 2	2 12
197	16	M.	4 21	7 19	14 58	0 19	10	20	1¾	2¼	feet	9 34	3 4
198	17	Tu.	4 22	7 18	14 56	0 21	10	21	2¾	3¼	h'd	10 4	3 56
199	18	W.	4 23	7 18	14 55	0 22	10	22	3½	4	h'd	10 37	4 47
200	19	Th.	4 24	7 17	14 53	0 24	10	23	4½	5	n'k	11 14	5 40
201	20	Fr.	4 24	7 16	14 52	0 25	10	24	5½	6	n'k	11 55	6 34
202	21	Sa.	4 25	7 15	14 50	0 27	10	25	6½	7	arm	morn	7 29
203	22	S.	4 26	7 14	14 48	0 29	10	26	7½	8	arm	0 43	8 24
204	23	M.	4 27	7 13	14 46	0 31	9	27	8½	8¾	br.	1 36	9 19
205	24	Tu.	4 28	7 12	14 44	0 33	9	28	9½	9¾	br.	2 35	10 13
206	25	W.	4 29	7 12	14 43	0 34	9	29	10½	10½	br.	3 36	11 4
207	26	Th.	4 30	7 11	14 41	0 36	9	●	11¼	11½	h'rt	**sets**	11 52
208	27	Fr.	4 31	7 10	14 39	0 38	9	1	—	0	h'rt	7 27	0 38
209	28	Sa.	4 32	7 8	14 36	0 41	9	2	0¼	0¾	bel.	7 53	1 21
210	29	S.	4 33	7 7	14 34	0 43	9	3	0¾	1¼	bel.	8 17	2 3
211	30	M.	4 34	7 6	14 32	0 45	9	4	1½	2	bel.	8 42	2 44
212	31	Tu.	4 35	7 5	14 30	0 47	10	5	2¼	2½	rei.	9 6	3 26

JULY hath 31 days. [1900

An oriental Sultan, July comes
  In all the glory of barbaric state,
While the bumblebees and locusts beat their drums,
  And shrill grasshoppers at his call await.

WALTER MALONE.

D. M.	D. W.	Aspects, Holidays, Events, Weather, Etc.	Farmer's Calendar.
1	G	3♄ Sunday after Trinity.	The old strawberry bed should be ploughed early in the month, and some late crop planted. Rutabaga, sweet corn, cucumber, bean and cabbage are good crops to grow after the first of July. The corn should be an early variety, also the bean.
2	M.	⊕ in Aphelion. *Fine*	
3	Tu.	☾ in Apog. 4th. ☿ in ♋.	
4	W.	INDEPEND. DAY. ☿ gr. el. E.	
5	Th.	Low tides.	
6	Fr.	{5th. John P. Newman, Metho. bishop, d. 1899, aged 73.	
7	Sa.	{6th. Robert Bonner, publisher, d. 1899, aged 75.	
8	G	4th Sun. af. Trin. ☌ ♃ ☾.	The farmer should make an effort to keep his crops clean of weeds, that he may not have to leave the mowing field to cultivate his crops when the grass needs to be cut. The old method of leaving the grass to stand until the seed is nearly ripe, is not a good one; it is now very generally conceded that grass should be cut when in full blossom. Under the old system of hand labor, many large farmers could not cut all of the grass at just the right time, but for want of a sufficiently large force of laborers, some of it had to be left uncut until the seed had ripened; but now with improved implements, one man can accomplish in one day what it formerly used to require several days to do with hand labor.
9	M.	☌ ♅ ☾. ♄ in Aphel. *with*	
10	Tu.	☾ runs low. ☌ ♄ ☾.	
11	W.	{8th. Geo. W. Julian, anti-slav. leader, d. 1899, aged 82.	
12	Th.	Med. tides. 8th. ☌ ♀ ☉ inf.	
13	Fr.	12th. Thoreau born, 1817, *showers.*	
14	Sa.	☿ in Aphel. 15th. ☾ Perig.	
15	G	5th Sun. af. Trin. St. Swithin.	
16	M.	{15th. W. A. Field, ch.-justice, Mass., d. 1899, aged 66.	
17	Tu.	☿ stationary. *Rain.*	
18	W.	22d. ☾ runs high.	
19	Th.	♂ in ♋.	
20	Fr.	St. Margaret. *Hot*	
21	Sa.	{21st. Robert G. Ingersoll d. 1899, aged about 67.	
22	G	6th ♋. af. Tr. St. Mary Magdalene.	Cattle at pasture should be looked after this month. If the weather be dry, feed will be short, and feeding at the barn will be required. The spring of water may get low and require digging deeper. And, as soon as feed gets short, the fences should be looked to, or the cattle will find some weak place to break through.
23	M.	☌ ♆ ☾, ♀ in Aphel. *and*	
24	Tu.	☌ ♀ ☾. 22d. ☌ ♂ ☾.	
25	W.	St. James. DOG-DAYS BEGIN.	
26	Th.	St. Anne. 25th. Medium tides.	
27	Fr.	☌ ☿ ☾.	
28	Sa.	{29th. Judge Geo. White, of Mass., d. 1899, aged 77. *dry.*	
29	G	7th Sun. aft. Trin. ♃ stat.	
30	M.	29th. ♀ stat. *Showers.*	
31	Tu.	☾ in Apog. Low tides.	

1900] AUGUST, Eighth Month.

ASTRONOMICAL CALCULATIONS.

⊙'s Declension. Days.	d. m.	Days.	d. m.	Days.	d. m.	Days.	d. m.	Days.	d. m.
1	18N.2	7	16 26	13	14 41	19	12 47	25	10 6
2	17 47	8	16 9	14	14 22	20	12 27	26	10 25
3	17 31	9	15 52	15	14 4	21	12 7	27	10 4
4	17 15	10	15 35	16	13 45	22	11 47	28	9 43
5	16 59	11	15 17	17	13 26	23	11 27	29	9 22
6	16 43	12	14 59	18	13 7	24	11 7	30	9 0

) First Quarter, 3d day, 11h. 46m., morning, E.
○ Full Moon, 10th day, 4h. 30m., evening, E.
(Last Quarter, 17th day, 6h. 46m., morning, W.
● New Moon, 24th day, 10h. 53m., evening, W.

Day of Year.	Day of Month.	Day of the Week.	⊙ Rises. h. m.	Sets. h. m.	Length of Days. h m.	Day's Decr. h. m.	Sun Fast m.	Moon's Age.	Full Sea, Boston. Morn h.	Even h.	) 's Place	) Rises. h. m.	) Souths. h. m.
213	1	W.	4 36	7 4	14 28	0 49	10	6	2¾	3¼	rei.	9 33	4 8
214	2	Th.	4 37	7 3	14 26	0 51	10	7	3½	4	sec.	10 2	4 52
215	3	Fr.	4 38	7 2	14 24	0 53	10	8	4¼	4¾	sec.	10 36	5 38
216	4	Sa.	4 39	7 1	14 22	0 55	10	9	5	5½	sec.	11 16	6 28
217	5	S.	4 40	6 59	14 19	0 58	10	10	6	6½	thi.	morn	7 20
218	6	M.	4 41	6 58	14 17	1 0	10	11	7	7¼	thi.	0 3	8 15
219	7	Tu.	4 42	6 57	14 15	1 2	10	12	8	8¼	kn.	0 59	9 11
220	8	W.	4 43	6 56	14 13	1 4	10	13	8¾	9¼	kn.	2 3	10 8
221	9	Th.	4 44	6 54	14 10	1 7	10	14	9¾	10	legs	3 12	11 4
222	10	Fr.	4 45	6 53	14 8	1 9	11	○	10½	11	legs	rises	11 59
223	11	Sa.	4 46	6 51	14 5	1 12	11	16	11½	11¾	feet	7 2	morn
224	12	S.	4 48	6 50	14 2	1 15	11	17	—	0¼	feet	7 34	0 54
225	13	M.	4 49	6 49	14 0	1 17	11	18	0½	1	h'd.	8 6	1 48
226	14	Tu.	4 50	6 47	13 57	1 20	11	19	1½	2	h'd.	8 38	2 41
227	15	W.	4 51	6 46	13 55	1 22	11	20	2¼	2¾	n'k.	9 15	3 35
228	16	Th.	4 52	6 44	13 52	1 25	12	21	3¼	3¾	n'k.	9 56	4 29
229	17	Fr.	4 53	6 43	13 50	1 27	12	22	4¼	4½	arm	10 42	5 25
230	18	Sa.	4 54	6 41	13 47	1 30	12	23	5¼	5½	arm	11 33	6 21
231	19	S.	4 55	6 40	13 45	1 32	12	24	6¼	6½	arm	morn	7 16
232	20	M.	4 56	6 38	13 42	1 35	12	25	7¼	7¾	br.	0 30	8 9
233	21	Tu.	4 57	6 37	13 40	1 37	13	26	8¼	8½	br.	1 29	9 0
234	22	W.	4 58	6 35	13 37	1 40	13	27	9¼	9½	h'rt	2 31	9 49
235	23	Th.	4 59	6 34	13 35	1 42	13	28	10	10¼	h'rt	3 32	10 35
236	24	Fr.	5 0	6 32	13 32	1 45	13	●	10¾	11	h'rt	sets	11 19
237	25	Sa	5 1	6 31	13 30	1 47	14	1	11½	11¾	bel.	6 22	0 1
238	26	S.	5 2	6 29	13 27	1 50	14	2	—	0¼	bel.	6 46	0 43
239	27	M.	5 3	6 27	13 24	1 53	14	3	0½	0¾	rei.	7 11	1 24
240	28	Tu.	5 5	6 26	13 21	1 56	15	4	1	1¼	rei.	7 37	2 6
241	29	W.	5 6	6 24	13 18	1 59	15	5	1¾	2	rei.	8 5	2 49
242	30	Th.	5 7	6 22	13 15	2 2	15	6	2¼	2¾	sec.	8 37	3 34
243	31	Fr.	5 8	6 21	13 13	2 4	15	7	3	3¼	sec.	9 14	4 21

AUGUST hath 31 days. [1900

The quiet August noon has come;
A slumberous silence fills the sky,
The fields are still, the woods are dumb,
In glassy sleep the waters lie. — BRYANT.

D. M.	D. W.	Aspects, Holidays, Events, Weather, Etc.	Farmer's Calendar.
1	W.	Lammas Day. ☌ ☿ ⊙ inf.	The month for weeds; yet too many farmers have the idea that most crops will require but little attention after the first of this month. The real fact is that all hoed crops which do not fully cover the ground, need cultivation during the entire growing season. Weeds grow more rapidly in August than in any other month, and it requires more persistent effort to kill them.
2	Th.	1st. The Pilgrims left Holland 1620.	
3	Fr.	☿ gr. hel. lat. S. *Hot*	
4	Sa.	Low tides.	
5	C	8th Sun. af. Trin. ☌ ♃ ☾.	
6	M.	Transfiguration. ☾ runs low.	
7	Tu.	☌ ♄ ☾, ☌ ♂ ♅. *with*	
8	W.	5th. ☌ ♅ ☾.	
9	Th.	8th. Hurricane, Porto Rico, 1899. 12th. Death of King Philip, 1676.	When the land is cleared of an early crop, and no second cultivated crop is to be grown, it should be ploughed, and three pecks of winter rye sown on each acre. This will not only prevent the weeds from growing, but will furnish a good green crop to plough under the following Spring.
10	Fr.	St. Lawrence. ☿ stat. *showers.*	
11	Sa.	High tides. {16th. Bat. of Bennington, 1777.	
12	C	9th Sun. af. Tr. ☾ in Perig.	
13	M.	{19th. Charles Endicott, Mass. Tax Com'r, d. 1899, aged 76.	
14	Tu.	♀ gr. brill. *Rain.*	
15	W.	Assump. of V. Mary. ♀ gr. h. l. S.	
16	Th.	{20th. Isaac McLellan, poet, d. 1899. aged 93.	From apple and pear trees that have more fruit set than they can fully mature, a portion should be picked off, or the fruit will be small and the trees in no condition to bear next year. To get any profit from an orchard, it is important to have fruit of the first quality; that of the second quality will frequently have to be sold for less than the cost of harvesting and marketing.
17	Fr.	♅ stationary. *Dry*	
18	Sa.	Med. tides. 19th. ☿ gr. el. W.	
19	C	10th Su. af. Tr. ☾ runs high.	
20	M.	☌ ♂ ☾. 19th. ☌ ♅ ☾.	
21	Tu.	☌ ♀ ☾. *and*	
22	W.	☿ in ☊.	
23	Th.	☌ ☿ ☾.	
24	Fr.	St. Bartholomew. *dusty.*	
25	Sa.	☐ ♃ ⊙.	Look after the trees and shrubs set last Spring; see that they are watered at least once a week during dry weather, and keep them well mulched with leaves or small evergreen branches. In watering, wet the ground as far as the roots extend.
26	C	11th Sunday after Trinity.	
27	M.	☾ in Apog., ☿ in Perihel.	
28	Tu.	St. Augustine. *Unsettled.*	
29	W.	Beheading of St. John Baptist.	
30	Th.	{24th. Ex-Judge Henry Hilton d. 1899, aged 74.	
31	Fr.	Low tides.	

1900] SEPTEMBER, Ninth Month.

ASTRONOMICAL CALCULATIONS.

☉'s Declination.

Days.	d. m.	Days.	d. m.	Days.	d. m.	Days.	d. m.	Days.	d. m.
1	8 N 17	7	6 4	13	3 48	19	1 29	25	0 52
2	7 55	8	5 42	14	3 25	20	1 5	26	1 15
3	7 33	9	5 19	15	3 2	21	0 42	27	1 38
4	7 11	10	4 56	16	2 38	22	0 N. 19	28	2 2
5	6 49	11	4 34	17	2 15	23	0 S. 5	29	2 25
6	6 27	12	4 11	18	1 52	24	0 28	30	2 48

☽ First Quarter, 2d day, 2h. 56m., morning, W.

○ Full Moon, 9th day, 0h. 6m., morning, W.

☾ Last Quarter, 15th day, 3h. 57m., evening, W.

● New Moon, 23d day, 2h. 57m., evening, W.

Day of Year.	Day of Month.	Day of the Week.	☉ Rises. h. m.	☉ Sets. h. m.	Length of Days. h. m.	Day's Decr. h. m.	Sun Fast m.	Moon's Age.	Full Sea, Boston. Morn h.	Full Sea, Boston. Even h.	☽'s Place	☽ Rises. h. m.	☽ Souths. h. m.
244	1	Sa.	5 9	6 19	13 10	2 7	16	8	3¾	4	thi.	9 57	5 11
245	2	S.	5 10	6 17	13 7	2 10	16	9	4½	5	thi.	10 47	6 3
246	3	M.	5 11	6 16	13 5	2 12	16	10	5½	5¾	kn.	11 45	6 57
247	4	Tu.	5 12	6 14	13 2	2 15	17	11	6½	6¾	kn.	morn	7 52
248	5	W.	5 13	6 12	12 59	2 18	17	12	7½	7¾	kn.	0 50	8 48
249	6	Th.	5 14	6 10	12 56	2 21	17	13	8½	8¾	legs	2 0	9 43
250	7	Fr.	5 15	6 9	12 54	2 23	18	14	9¼	9¾	legs	3 15	10 38
251	8	Sa.	5 16	6 7	12 51	2 26	18	15	10¼	10½	feet	4 31	11 33
252	9	S.	5 17	6 5	12 48	2 29	18	○	11	11½	feet	**rises**	morn
253	10	M.	5 18	6 4	12 46	2 31	19	17	11¾	—	h'd	6 36	0 27
254	11	Tu.	5 19	6 2	12 43	2 34	19	18	0¼	0¾	h'd	7 12	1 23
255	12	W.	5 20	6 0	12 40	2 37	19	19	1	1½	n'k	7 53	2 19
256	13	Th.	5 21	5 58	12 37	2 40	20	20	2	2¼	n'k	8 38	3 16
257	14	Fr.	5 22	5 56	12 34	2 43	20	21	2¾	3¼	arm	9 30	4 14
258	15	Sa.	5 24	5 55	12 31	2 46	21	22	3¾	4¼	arm	10 26	5 10
259	16	S.	5 25	5 53	12 28	2 49	21	23	4¾	5¼	br.	11 25	6 5
260	17	M.	5 26	5 51	12 25	2 52	21	24	6	6¼	br.	morn	6 57
261	18	Tu.	5 27	5 49	12 22	2 55	22	25	7	7¼	h'rt	0 25	7 47
262	19	W.	5 28	5 48	12 20	2 57	22	26	8	8¼	h'rt	1 26	8 33
263	20	Th.	5 29	5 46	12 17	3 0	22	27	9	9¼	h'rt	2 27	9 17
264	21	Fr.	5 30	5 44	12 14	3 3	23	28	9¾	10	bel.	3 26	10 0
265	22	Sa.	5 31	5 42	12 11	3 6	23	29	10¼	10¾	bel.	4 25	10 42
266	23	S.	5 32	5 41	12 9	3 8	23	●	11	11¼	rei.	**sets**	11 23
267	24	M.	5 33	5 39	12 6	3 11	24	1	11½	—	rei.	5 42	0 5
268	25	Tu.	5 34	5 37	12 3	3 14	24	2	0	0¼	rei.	6 9	0 47
269	26	W.	5 35	5 35	12 0	3 17	24	3	0½	0¾	sec.	6 39	1 31
270	27	Th.	5 36	5 33	11 57	3 20	25	4	1¼	1½	sec.	7 14	2 18
271	28	Fr.	5 38	5 32	11 54	3 23	25	5	1¾	2	thi.	7 55	3 6
272	29	Sa.	5 39	5 30	11 51	3 26	25	6	2½	2¾	thi.	8 42	3 57
273	30	S.	5 40	5 28	11 48	3 29	26	7	3¼	3½	thi.	9 35	4 49

SEPTEMBER hath 30 days. [1900

Sweet day, so cool, so calm, so bright,
The bridal of the earth and sky,
Sweet dews shall weep thy fall tonight, —
For thou must die! — GEO. HERBERT.

D. M.	D. W.	Aspects, Holidays, Events, Weather, Etc.	Farmer's Calendar.
1	Sa.	□ ♅ ☉, ☾ ♃ ☾. 2ᵈ· ☾ r. l.	Modern farmers find it for their interest to dig their potatoes as early this month as they become large enough to send to market; the prices are, as a rule, higher the first of the month than at a later period. If the crop can be harvested before the middle of the month, grass-seed can be sown to good advantage, if it be desired to sow the land down to grass; or, if the land should be wanted for cultivated crops the following year, the ground can be ploughed, and a crop of winter rye grown for fodder to be cut next spring, or a green crop can be raised to plough under before planting time. It pays well to keep the ground covered with some green crop during the fall and winter. Gather your best fruits and vegetables to exhibit at the Agricultural Fair, and encourage your wife to gather flowers from her garden to make a display of cut flowers; then with your whole family go to the fair to see where you stand when compared with your neighbors. If their exhibits are better than yours, resolve to surpass them next year. Do not attribute your want of success to ill luck. On the other hand, do not get discouraged. Study to find if there was not some error of judgment or otherwise, which you may avoid repeating in future. And keep trying until you grow as good products as the most skilful of your competitors.
2	G	12th. Su. af. Tr. ☾ ♅ ☾.	
3	M.	LABOR DAY. L. tide. ☾ ♄ ☾.	
4	Tu.	2ᵈ· ♄ stat. {4th. Election in Vermont.	
5	W.	DOG-DAYS END. *Pleasant*	
6	Th.	☿ gr. hel. lat. N. *weather.*	
7	Fr.	{8th. Rear-Adm. H. P. Picking, d. 1899, aged 59.	
8	Sa.	Nativity of V. Mary. *Cooler.*	
9	G	13th Su. af. Tr. ☾ in Perig.	
10	M.	8th. Bat. of Lake George, 1755.	
11	Tu.	High tides.	
12	W.	10th. Election in Maine. 16th. Anne Bradstreet d. 1672.	
13	Th.	☾ ☿ ☉ sup. *A*	
14	Fr.	17th. Rev. John Hall d. 1898, aged 69.	
15	Sa.	☾ runs high.	
16	G	14th Su. af. Tr. ☾ ♆ ☾.	
17	M.	♀ gr. elong. W. *storm*	
18	Tu.	Low tides. ☾ ♂ ☾. *is*	
19	W.	☾ ♀ ☾. *due.*	
20	Th.	17-19. R.R. Jubilee in Boston, 1851.	
21	Fr.	St. Matthew. 23ᵈ· ☾ in Apog.	
22	Sa.	□ ♄ ☉, □ ♆ ☉.	
23	G	15th S. af. Tr. ☉ en. ♎ {Aut. beg.}	
24	M.	Medium tides. ☾ ☿ ☾.	
25	Tu.	22d. John Alden d. 1687. aged 87. 22d. Nathan Hale executed, 1776.	
26	W.	30th. Br. war vessels arr. in Boston, 1768.	
27	Th.	29th· ☾ ♅ ☾, ☿ in ♋.	
28	Fr.	30th· ☾ ♄ ☾. ☾ runs low.	
29	Sa.	St. Michael and all Angels. ☾ ♃ ☾.	
30	G	16th S. a. T. St. Jerome. *Frost.*	

1900] OCTOBER, TENTH MONTH.

ASTRONOMICAL CALCULATIONS.

☉'s Declination.

Days.	d. m.	Days.	d. m.	Days.	d. m.	Days.	d. m.	Days.	d. m.
1	3s. 12	7	5 31	13	7 47	19	10 0	25	12 7
2	3 35	8	5 54	14	8 10	20	10 21	26	12 28
3	3 58	9	6 17	15	8 32	21	10 43	27	12 48
4	4 21	10	6 39	16	8 54	22	11 4	28	13 8
5	4 45	11	7 2	17	9 16	23	11 25	29	13 28
6	5 8	12	7 25	18	9 38	24	11 46	30	13 48

☽ First Quarter, 1st day, 4h. 11m., evening, E.
○ Full Moon, 8th day, 8h. 18m., morning, W.
☾ Last Quarter, 15th day, 4h. 51m., morning, E.
● New Moon, 23d day, 8h. 27m., morning, E.
☽ First Quarter, 31st day, 3h., 18m., morning, W.

Day of Year.	Day of Month.	Day of the Week.	☉ Rises. h. m.	☉ Sets. h. m.	Length of Days. h. m.	Day's Decr. h. m.	Sun Fast m.	Moon's Age.	Full Sea, Boston. Morn h.	Full Sea, Boston. Even h.	☽'s Place	☽ Sets. h. m.	☽ Souths. h. m.
274	1	M.	5 41	5 26	11 45	3 32	26	8	4	4½	kn.	10 35	5 42
275	2	Tu.	5 42	5 25	11 43	3 34	26	9	5	5½	kn.	11 41	6 35
276	3	W.	5 43	5 23	11 40	3 37	27	10	6	6½	legs	morn	7 29
277	4	Th.	5 44	5 21	11 37	3 40	27	11	7	7½	legs	0 51	8 22
278	5	Fr.	5 45	5 19	11 34	3 43	27	12	8	8½	feet	2 3	9 15
279	6	Sa.	5 47	5 18	11 31	3 46	28	13	9	9¼	feet	3 18	10 10
280	7	S.	5 48	5 16	11 28	3 49	28	14	9¾	10¼	h'd	4 35	11 5
281	8	M.	5 49	5 14	11 25	3 52	28	○	10¾	11	h'd	**rises**	morn
282	9	Tu.	5 50	5 13	11 23	3 54	28	16	11½	—	n'k	5 44	0 2
283	10	W.	5 51	5 11	11 20	3 57	29	17	0	0¼	n'k	6 29	1 0
284	11	Th.	5 52	5 10	11 18	3 59	29	18	0¾	1	arm	7 20	1 59
285	12	Fr.	5 53	5 8	11 15	4 2	29	19	1¾	2	arm	8 16	2 59
286	13	Sa.	5 54	5 6	11 12	4 5	29	20	2½	2¾	br.	9 16	3 56
287	14	S.	5 55	5 5	11 10	4 7	30	21	3½	3¾	br.	10 17	4 51
288	15	M.	5 56	5 3	11 7	4 10	30	22	4½	4¾	br.	11 19	5 42
289	16	Tu.	5 57	5 1	11 4	4 13	30	23	5½	5¾	h'rt	morn	6 30
290	17	W.	5 59	5 0	11 1	4 16	30	24	6½	6¾	h'rt	0 20	7 16
291	18	Th.	6 0	4 58	10 58	4 19	30	25	7½	7¾	bel.	1 20	7 59
292	19	Fr.	6 2	4 57	10 55	4 22	31	26	8¼	8¾	bel.	2 19	8 41
293	20	Sa.	6 3	4 55	10 52	4 25	31	27	9¼	9½	bel.	3 17	9 22
294	21	S.	6 4	4 53	10 49	4 28	31	28	9¾	10¼	rei.	4 15	10 3
295	22	M.	6 5	4 52	10 47	4 30	31	29	10½	10¾	rei.	5 13	10 46
296	23	Tu.	6 6	4 50	10 44	4 33	31	●	11	11½	sec.	**sets**	11 30
297	24	W.	6 8	4 49	10 41	4 36	31	1	11¾	—	sec.	5 16	0 16
298	25	Th.	6 9	4 48	10 39	4 38	32	2	0	0¼	sec.	5 55	1 4
299	26	Fr.	6 10	4 46	10 36	4 41	32	3	0¾	1	thi.	6 40	1 53
300	27	Sa.	6 11	4 45	10 34	4 43	32	4	1¼	1½	thi.	7 31	2 45
301	28	S.	6 12	4 43	10 31	4 46	32	5	2	2¼	kn.	8 29	3 37
302	29	M.	6 14	4 42	10 28	4 49	32	6	2¾	3¼	kn.	9 31	4 29
303	30	Tu.	6 15	4 41	10 26	4 51	32	7	3¾	4	legs	10 37	5 21
304	31	W.	6 16	4 39	10 23	4 54	32	8	4¾	5	legs	11 46	6 12

OCTOBER hath 31 days. [1900

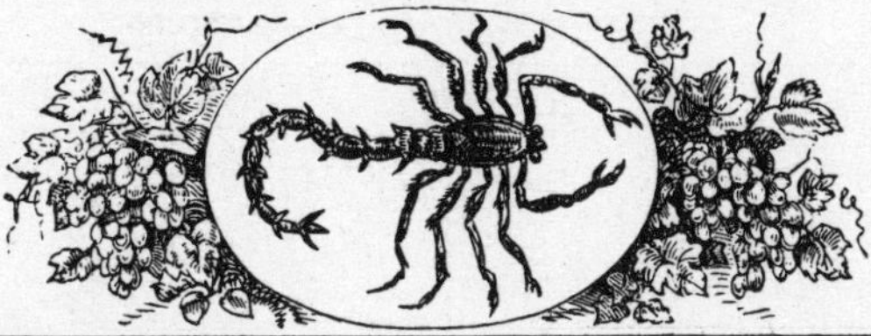

Heaven's inmost warmth may wait us still.
What if, beyond time's autumn chill,
There bless us, ere we hence depart,
A glad October of the heart! — LUCY LARCOM.

D. M.	D. W.	Aspects, Holidays, Events, Weather, Etc.	Farmer's Calendar.
1	M.	7th. First Mass. Prov. Congress, 1774.	Apples and pears should all be gathered early in this month, and if of late keeping varieties, pack them at once in barrels or boxes, and place them in a cool, dry cellar where the temperature will vary but little from eight degrees above the freezing point of water. In such a place they should be kept until wanted for use, or for sale. To change the air or temperature will hasten decay; which is a fact that many of the past generation failed to learn. Fruit put up for home use should be put in boxes holding about one bushel each, having a cover on hinges, so the fruit can be easily examined by opening the box, or a portion of the fruit taken out without disturbing the remainder.
2	Tu.	Low tides. ♆ stat. *Clear*	
3	W.	{7th. Sherman Hoar, ex-M.C. f'm Mass., { d. 1898, aged 38.	
4	Th.	8th. John Hancock d. 1793, aged 55.	
5	Fr.	10th. Rev. John Cotton arr. in Bost. 1633.	
6	Sa.	11th. Vermont legislature meets. 12th. John M. Forbes d. 1898, aged 85.	
7	G	17th Sunday after Trinity.	
8	M.	☽ in Perigee. *and*	
9	Tu.	St. Denis. High tides. *cold.*	
10	W.	☿ in Aphelion, ♀ in ☍.	
11	Th.	17th. Bat. of Saratoga, 1777. 18th. U. S. take poss. of Porto Rico, 1898.	
12	Fr.	☽ runs high.	
13	Sa.	☌ ♆ ☽. *A*	
14	G	18th Sunday after Trinity.	Chrysanthemums for November exhibition should be well cared for during September and October, and housed as soon as the weather becomes too cool for a vigorous growth. During the last of this month the soil should be well prepared for early flowering bulbs. Before planting the bulbs, the surface of the ground should be made much higher in the middle of each plot, so that the water will drain off rapidly. The soil for early flowering bulbs should be made very fine, and in planting the bulbs, arrange colors to secure the most pleasing effect. If the pullets are to lay before cold weather comes, they must have a warm house, and plenty to eat.
15	M.	{19th. Harold Frederic, Am. journalist, { d. 1898. aged 42.	
16	Tu.	☌ ♂ ☽. *storm*	
17	W.	Low tides.	
18	Th.	St. Luke, Evangelist. *coming.*	
19	Fr.	☌ ♀ ☽, ☌ ♃ ♅	
20	Sa.	{21st. Frigate "Constitution" { launched, 1797.	
21	G	19th Su. af. Tr. ☽ in Apog.	
22	M.	{29th. G. E. Waring, jr., civ. engineer, { d. 1898, aged 65.	
23	Tu.	{30th. Gov. John A. Andrew, Mass., { d. 1867, aged 49.	
24	W.	28th. ☌ ♄ ☽	
25	Th.	St. Crispin. ☌ ☿ ☽. *Fine*	
26	Fr.	M. tides. ☌ ♅ ☽, ☌ ♃ ☽.	
27	Sa.	☽ runs low. *with*	
28	G	20th Su. af. Tr. St. Simon and	
29	M.	☿ gr. elong. E. [St. Jude.	
30	Tu	☿ gr. hel. lat. S.	
31	W.	All Hallows Eve. *frosts.*	

1900] NOVEMBER, Eleventh Month.

ASTRONOMICAL CALCULATIONS.

☉'s Declination.	Days.	d. m.	Days.	d. m.	Days.	d. m.	Days.	d. m.	Days.	d. m.
	1	14s. 27	7	16 18	13	17 59	19	19 29	25	20 46
	2	14 46	8	16 36	14	18 15	20	19 43	26	20 58
	3	15 5	9	16 53	15	18 30	21	19 56	27	21 9
	4	15 24	10	17 10	16	18 46	22	20 9	28	21 20
	5	15 42	11	17 27	17	19 0	23	20 22	29	21 30
	6	16 0	12	17 43	18	19 15	24	20 34	30	21 40

○ Full Moon, 6th day, 6h. 0m., evening, E.

☾ Last Quarter, 13th day, 9h. 38m., evening, E.

● New Moon, 22d day, 2h. 17m., morning, E.

☽ First Quarter, 29th day, 0h. 35m., evening, E.

Day of Year.	Day of Month.	Day of the Week.	☉ Rises. h. m.	☉ Sets. h. m.	Length of Days. h. m.	Day's Decr. h. m.	Sun Fast m.	Moon's Age.	Full Sea, Boston. Morn h.	Full Sea, Boston. Even h.	☽'s Place	☽ Sets. h. m.	☽ Souths. h. m.
305	1	Th.	6 17	4 38	10 21	4 56	32	9	5¾	6	feet	morn	7 4
306	2	Fr.	6 19	4 37	10 18	4 59	32	10	6½	7	feet	0 57	7 55
307	3	Sa.	6 20	4 36	10 16	5 1	32	11	7½	8	feet	2 10	8 48
308	4	S.	6 21	4 34	10 13	5 4	32	12	8½	9	h'd	3 24	9 43
309	5	M.	6 22	4 33	10 11	5 6	32	13	9¼	10	h'd	4 40	10 40
310	6	Tu.	6 23	4 32	10 9	5 8	32	○	10¼	10¾	n'k	**rises**	11 39
311	7	W.	6 25	4 31	10 6	5 11	32	15	11¼	11¾	n'k	5 4	morn
312	8	Th.	6 26	4 30	10 4	5 13	32	16	—	0	arm	5 59	0 40
313	9	Fr.	6 27	4 29	10 2	5 15	32	17	0½	0¾	arm	6 59	1 40
314	10	Sa.	6 28	4 28	10 0	5 17	32	18	1¼	1½	br.	8 2	2 38
315	11	S.	6 30	4 27	9 57	5 20	32	19	2¼	2½	br.	9 7	3 33
316	12	M.	6 31	4 26	9 55	5 22	31	20	3	3¼	h'rt	10 10	4 23
317	13	Tu.	6 32	4 25	9 53	5 24	31	21	4	4¼	h'rt	11 11	5 11
318	14	W.	6 33	4 24	9 51	5 26	31	22	5	5¼	bel.	morn	5 55
319	15	Th.	6 35	4 23	9 48	5 29	31	23	6	6¼	bel.	0 10	6 38
320	16	Fr.	6 36	4 22	9 46	5 31	31	24	6¾	7¼	bel.	1 9	7 19
321	17	Sa.	6 37	4 21	9 44	5 33	31	25	7¾	8	rei.	2 7	8 1
322	18	S.	6 38	4 20	9 42	5 35	30	26	8½	8¾	rei.	3 5	8 43
323	19	M.	6 40	4 20	9 40	5 37	30	27	9¼	9½	sec.	4 4	9 26
324	20	Tu.	6 41	4 19	9 38	5 39	30	28	9¾	10¼	sec.	5 3	10 12
325	21	W.	6 42	4 18	9 36	5 41	30	29	10½	11	sec.	6 2	10 59
326	22	Th.	6 43	4 17	9 34	5 43	29	●	11¼	11½	thi.	**sets**	11 49
327	23	Fr.	6 44	4 16	9 32	5 45	29	1	11¾	—	thi.	5 27	0 41
328	24	Sa.	6 46	4 16	9 30	5 47	29	2	0¼	0½	kn.	6 23	1 33
329	25	S.	6 47	4 15	9 28	5 49	29	3	1	1¼	kn.	7 25	2 26
330	26	M.	6 48	4 15	9 27	5 50	28	4	1¾	2	kn.	8 30	3 18
331	27	Tu.	6 49	4 14	9 25	5 52	28	5	2½	2¾	legs	9 37	4 9
332	28	W.	6 50	4 14	9 24	5 53	28	6	3½	3¾	legs	10 46	4 59
333	29	Th.	6 52	4 14	9 22	5 55	27	7	4¼	4¾	feet	11 56	5 49
334	30	Fr.	6 53	4 13	9 20	5 57	27	8	5¼	5¾	feet	morn	6 40

NOVEMBER hath 30 days. [1900

From gold to gray
Our mild, sweet day
Of Indian summer fades too soon;
But tenderly
Above the sea
Hangs, white and calm, the hunter's moon. — WHITTIER.

D. M.	D. W.	Aspects, Holidays, Events, Weather, Etc.	Farmer's Calendar.
1	Th.	All Saints' Day. *A*	Prepare for winter in the early part of this month. All tender plants and shrubs should be well protected with mats or straw, or evergreen boughs and leaves. Water pipes should be protected with dry saw dust or hair packing, and boxed so as to keep the packing dry. Windows should be repaired; doors made to shut tight, and cellar walls protected from the cold. A few days spent during the first week of this month preparing for the coldest winter weather will often save what could not be purchased by weeks of labor. Never wait for a heavy snow storm before buying a sled, or until it rains before buying an umbrella. Prepare as far as possible for coming events. Get the young cattle home before the ground is covered with snow; and provide them with good winter quarters. The sheep also should be well housed before winter sets in; better get them home two weeks before snow comes, than to have them out in a single cold storm. The wise farmer will have plenty of sheds open to the south where his sheep and cattle can be kept comfortable in the warmest part of the day during the winter. All farm animals need good air and plenty of sunshine if they are to be kept in good health. Give the laying hens warm quarters, with pure air and plenty of sunshine; keep them well supplied with good feed.
2	Fr.	1st. Stamp Act took effect, 1765.	
3	Sa.	{5th. David A. Wells, polit.-economist, d. 1898, aged 70.	
4	C	21st Sunday after Trinity.	
5	M.	☾ in Perigee. *cold*	
6	Tu.	High tides. {6th. Presidential election.	
7	W.	{6th. State elections in N. H., Mass. and Conn.	
8	Th.	{16th. Samuel C. Bartlett, ex-pres. Dartmouth Coll., d. 1898, aged 81.	
9	Fr.	☌ ♆ ☿, ☿ stat. *rain.*	
10	Sa.	9th. ☾ runs high.	
11	C	22d Su. af. Tr. St. Martin.	
12	M.	11th. Medium tides.	
13	Tu.	♀ in Perihelion. *Clear*	
14	W.	☌ ♂ ☾.	
15	Th.	{24th. Col. Henry Lee, Boston, d. 1898, aged 81.	
16	Fr.	Low tides.	
17	Sa.	☾ in Apogee. *for*	
18	C	23d Su. af. Tr. ☿ in ♋.	
19	M.	18th. ☌ ♀ ☾. *some*	
20	Tu.	☌ ☿ ⊙ inf. [inv.	
21	W.	☌ ☿ ☾. 21–2. Ann. ecl. ⊙,	
22	Th.	St. Cecilia. □ ♂ ⊙. *days.*	
23	Fr.	☌ ♅ ☾, ☿ in Per., ☌ ♃ ☾.	
24	Sa.	☌ ♄ ☾. 22d. M. tides. *Rain*	
25	C	24th Su. af. Tr. St. Catherine.	
26	M.	23d. ☾ runs low. *or*	
27	Tu.	{26-7th. Great and fatal storm, 1898. *snow.*	
28	W.	{28th. Spain accepts our terms, 1898. *Blustering*	
29	Th.	☿ stationary.	
30	Fr.	St. Andrew. *weather.*	

1900] DECEMBER, Twelfth Month.

ASTRONOMICAL CALCULATIONS.

☉'s Declination.	Days.	d. m.	Days.	d. m.	Days.	d. m.	Days.	d. m.	Days.	d. m.
	1	21s. 49	7	22 38	13	23 10	19	23 25	25	23 24
	2	21 59	8	22 44	14	23 14	20	23 26	26	23 22
	3	22 7	9	22 50	15	23 17	21	23 27	27	23 20
	4	22 15	10	22 56	16	23 20	22	23 27	28	23 17
	5	22 23	11	23 1	17	23 22	23	23 27	29	23 14
	6	22 31	12	23 6	18	23 24	24	23 26	30	23 10

○ Full Moon, 6th day, 5h. 38m., morning, W.
☾ Last Quarter, 13th day, 5h. 42m., evening, E.
● New Moon, 21st day, 7h. 1m., evening, W.
☽ First Quarter, 28th day, 8h. 48m., evening, W.

Day of Year.	Day of Month.	Day of the Week.	☉ Rises. h. m.	☉ Sets. h. m.	Length of Days. h. m.	Day's Decr. h. m.	Sun Fast m.	Moon's Age.	Full Sea, Boston. Morn h.	Full Sea, Boston. Even h.	☽'s Place	☽ Sets. h. m.	☽ Souths, h. m.
335	1	Sa.	6 54	4 13	9 19	5 58	27	9	6¼	6¾	h'd	1 6	7 31
336	2	S.	6 55	4 12	9 17	6 0	26	10	7¼	7¾	h'd	2 19	8 25
337	3	M.	6 56	4 12	9 16	6 1	26	11	8	8¾	n'k	3 32	9 22
338	4	Tu.	6 57	4 12	9 15	6 2	25	12	9	9½	n'k	4 46	10 21
339	5	W.	6 58	4 12	9 14	6 3	25	13	10	10½	arm	5 57	11 21
340	6	Th.	6 59	4 12	9 13	6 4	25	○	10¾	11¼	arm	**rises**	morn
341	7	Fr.	7 0	4 12	9 12	6 5	24	15	11¾	—	br.	5 42	0 20
342	8	Sa.	7 1	4 12	9 11	6 6	24	16	0¼	0½	br.	6 47	1 17
343	9	S.	7 2	4 12	9 10	6 7	23	17	1	1¼	h'rt	7 52	2 11
344	10	M.	7 3	4 12	9 9	6 8	23	18	1¾	2	h'rt	8 56	3 2
345	11	Tu.	7 4	4 12	9 8	6 9	22	19	2¾	3	h'rt	9 58	3 48
346	12	W.	7 4	4 12	9 8	6 9	22	20	3½	3¾	bel.	10 58	4 33
347	13	Th.	7 5	4 12	9 7	6 10	21	21	4¼	4¾	bel.	11 56	5 15
348	14	Fr.	7 6	4 12	9 6	6 11	21	22	5¼	5½	rei.	morn	5 57
349	15	Sa.	7 6	4 12	9 6	6 11	20	23	6	6½	rei.	0 54	6 38
350	16	S.	7 7	4 13	9 6	6 11	20	24	7	7¼	rei.	1 53	7 21
351	17	M.	7 8	4 13	9 5	6 12	19	25	7¾	8¼	sec.	2 52	8 6
352	18	Tu.	7 9	4 14	9 5	6 12	19	26	8½	9	sec.	3 51	8 52
353	19	W.	7 10	4 14	9 4	6 13	18	27	9¼	9¾	thi.	4 50	9 41
354	20	Th.	7 10	4 14	9 4	6 13	18	28	10	10½	thi.	5 47	10 33
355	21	Fr.	7 11	4 15	9 4	Inc.	18	●	10¾	11¼	thi.	**sets**	11 26
356	22	Sa.	7 11	4 15	9 4	0 0	17	1	11¼	11¾	kn.	5 14	0 20
357	23	S.	7 12	4 16	9 4	0 0	16	2	—	0	kn.	6 20	1 13
358	24	M.	7 12	4 17	9 5	0 1	16	3	0½	0¾	legs	7 28	2 6
359	25	Tu.	7 12	4 17	9 5	0 1	15	4	1¼	1¾	legs	8 37	2 57
360	26	W.	7 12	4 18	9 6	0 2	15	5	2¼	2½	feet	9 47	3 47
361	27	Th.	7 13	4 19	9 6	0 2	14	6	3	3¼	feet	10 57	4 37
362	28	Fr.	7 13	4 19	9 6	0 2	14	7	4	4¼	h'd	morn	5 27
363	29	Sa.	7 13	4 20	9 7	0 3	13	8	4¾	5¼	h'd	0 8	6 19
364	30	S.	7 14	4 21	9 7	0 3	13	9	5¾	6¼	n'k	1 19	7 13
365	31	M.	7 14	4 22	9 8	0 4	13	10	6¾	7¼	n'k	2 30	8 9

DECEMBER hath 31 days. [1900

Fading like a fading ember,
Last of all the shrunk December.
Him regarding, men remember,
Life and joy must pass away.—Austin Dobson.

D. M.	D. W.	Aspects, Holidays, Events, Weather, Etc.
1	Sa.	Medium tides. {2d. John Brown hanged, 1859.
2	G	1st. Sunday in Advent.
3	M.	☾ in Perig. ☿ gr. h. lat N.
4	Tu.	♀ gr. hel. lat. N. *Pleasant*
5	W.	☌ ♅ ☉. 6th. ☾ runs high.
6	Th.	St. Nicholas. High tides. *for*
7	Fr.	☌ ♆ ☾, ☿ gr. elong. W.
8	Sa.	{10th. Wm. Black, English novelist, d. 1898, aged 57. *some*
9	G	2d Sunday in Advent. *days.*
10	M.	{11th. Gen. Garcia, Cuban patriot, d. 1898, aged 62.
11	Tu.	{12th. Sir Wm. Jenner, Eng. physician, d. 1898, aged 83.
12	W.	☌ ♂ ☾. {15th. Ex-Sen. C. S. Brice, Ohio, d. 1898, aged 53.
13	Th.	{21st. E. S. Barrett, president of S. A. R., d. 1898, aged 65.
14	Fr.	☌ ♃ ☉. *Snow.*
15	Sa.	☾ in Apogee.
16	G	3d Sun. in Ad. Low tides.
17	M.	{28th. Sen. J. S. Morrill, Vt., d. 1898, aged 89.
18	Tu.	{30th. Senor Romero, Mexican minister, d. 1898, aged 62.
19	W.	☌ ♀ ☾, ☍ ♆ ☉.
20	Th.	☾ r. low. ☌ ☿ ☾, ☌ ♅ ☾.
21	Fr.	St. Thomas. ☌ ♃ ☾. {Winter begins.}
22	Sa.	☉ ent. ♑. ☌ ♄ ☾. *Clear*
23	G	4th Sunday in Advent.
24	M.	High tides. 22d. ☌ ☿ ♅.
25	Tu.	Christmas Day. *and*
26	W.	St. Stephen. ☿ in ☋. *cold.*
27	Th.	St. John Ev. {22d. Forefathers' Day first celeb., 1769.
28	Fr.	Holy Innocents. *Stormy.*
29	Sa.	☌ ♄ ☉. 30th. Med. tides.
30	G	1st Su. af. Chr. ☾ in Peri.
31	M.	30th. ☌ ☿ ♃.

Farmer's Calendar.

Again we come to the closing month of the year. Fortunate indeed is he who can look back and feel reasonably sure that no mistakes have been made during the past year, that could have been avoided. Whatever mistakes have been made, should make us better prepared to avoid making similar ones the coming year. The wise man looks back that he may be better prepared for future action; every failure should teach us to be better able to succeed in the next trial. Hope, courage and an untiring perseverance will enable us to conquer, when by the lack of these we should fail.

There is no better time to settle business accounts than at the close of the year. It may not be possible to settle them all but upon those that remain open we can ascertain just how much we owe and just how much is due us, and can strike the balance. Make both debits and credits as small as possible. Short accounts make long friends, but long accounts often make bitter enemies.

While the poor should never be forgotten, they should be particularly remembered at the close of the year by those who are blessed with ample means.

COLLEGES, PROFESSIONAL AND NORMAL SCHOOLS IN NEW ENGLAND.
(Corrected September, 1899.)

Colleges.

BATES, LEWISTON, ME. 3 tms. Beg. Sept. 12, Jan. 19, Apr. 10. Com. June 28, 1900.

BOWDOIN, BRUNSWICK, ME. Com. June 28, 1900. Vac. 11 w. fm. Com.; 2 w. at Christmas ; 1w. in Spring.

COLBY, WATERVILLE, ME. Com. Wed. bef. 4th of July. Tms : 1st, Sept. 20–Dec. 20 ; 2d, Jan. 3–Mar. 14 ; 3d, Mar. 28–June 27.

ME. WESLEYAN SEM. AND FEM. COL., KENT'S HILL, ME. 3t. Fall and Spring, 13w. ea. ; Winter, 12w. Aug 29, '99 ; Dec. 12, '99 ; Mar. 20, to Com. June 10–14, 1900.

UNIVERSITY OF MAINE, ORONO, ME. Tms. begin 3d Wed. in Sept. and Jan. Com. 2d Wed. in June.

DARTMOUTH, HANOVER, N.H. Com. last Wed. June ; vac. 11 w. after.

N.H. CONF. SEMINARY AND FEMALE COLLEGE, TILTON, N.H. 3 tms. Beg. Sept. 5, '99 ; Jan. 2, 1900 ; Apr. 3, 1900.

NORWICH UNIV. (Military), NORTH-FIELD, VT. Year beg. Th. Sept. 21, '99, closes June 29, 1900.

MIDDLEBURY, MIDDLEBURY, VT. Tms. beg. Jan. 9, Apr. 12, Sept. 20, 1900.

UNIVERSITY OF VT. AND STATE AG. COL., AT BURLINGTON. Com. last Wed. June ; vac. fm. Com. to last Wed. Sept.; fm Wed. bef. Chr'mas, 10d. ; 10d. in Apr.

MONTPELIER SEMINARY, MONTPE-LIER, VT. Tms. beg. Sept 5, and Dec. 12, '99 ; Mar. 20, 1900.

AMHERST, AMHERST, MASS. 3 tms. Beg. Jan. 4, Apr. 12, and Sept. 20, 1900.

BOSTON COLLEGE, BOSTON, MASS. 2 terms. Beg. Sept. 12, '99, and Feb. 3, 1900.

BOSTON UNIVER., BOSTON, MASS. — COLL. OF LIBERAL ARTS. 3 tms. 1st beg. Sept. 27, '99 ; 2d beg. Jan. 3, 1900 ; 3d beg. Mar. 21, 1900. GRADUATE SCH. OF ARTS AND SCI. Tms. as in Coll. of Lib. Arts.

CLARK UNIV., WORCESTER, MASS. Tms. beg. Sept. 28, '99, Jan. 1, 1900.

COLL. OF THE HOLY CROSS, WORCES-TER, MASS. Year beg. 1st Wed. Sept. 1899 ; ends June 21, 1900.

HARVARD UNIVERS., CAMBRIDGE, MASS. Year beg. Th. after last Wed. Sept., ends at Com. last Wed. June; recess Dec. 23 to Jan. 2, inclu., and 1w., including Apr. 19.

HARVARD GRAD. SCH., same as Uni.

MT. HOLYOKE COLL., So. HADLEY, MASS. (Women.) 3 tms. Sept. 14, '99 ; Jan. 4, Apr. 12, 1900. Com. June 20, 1900.

RADCLIFFE COLLEGE, CAMBRIDGE, MASS. (Women.) Year beg. Th. after last Wed. Sept.; recess Dec. 23 to Jan. 2, inclu., and Apr. 16, to 22, inclu.

SMITH COLL., NORTHAMPTON, MASS. (Wom.) 2 tms. 1st tm. beg. Sept. 21, '99.

TUFTS COLLEGE, MASS. Beg. Sept. 21, '99. Com. 3d Wed. June.

WELLESLEY COLLEGE, WELLESLEY, MASS. (Women.) 3 tms. Sept. 20, '99, Jan. 11, 1900, Apr. 17, 1900. Com. June 26.

WILLIAMS, WILLIAMSTOWN, MASS. Year beg. Sept. 21, '99. Com. June 20, 1900.

BROWN, PROVIDENCE, R.I. Acad. yr. beg. 3d Wed. Sept. Com. 3d Wed. June.

TRINITY, HARTFORD, CONN. 2 tms. 1st beg. Sept. 19, '99 ; 2d, Feb. 7, 1900. Com. last Wed. in June.

WESLEYAN UNIV., MIDDLETOWN, CT. Com. last Wed. in June; vac. 13w. fm. Com., 10d. at Chris., 5d. in Spring.

YALE UNIV., NEW HAVEN, CONN. Com. last Wed. in June; vac. 13w. fm. Com. 1st tm. 12w., vac. 2w.; 2d tm. till Com., with recess at Easter.

SCHOOL OF THE FINE ARTS (YALE UNIV.). Beg. Oct. 2, and ends June 1.

Theological Schools.

THEO. SEM., BANGOR, ME. (Or. Cong.). Anniver, 3d Wed. May; vac. 15w. fm. anniv. Ex. for entrance 1st Wed. Sept.

COBB DIVIN. SCH. OF BATES COLL., LEWISTON, ME. Beg. Sept. 13, cl. Dec. 22, '99 ; beg. Jan. 2, 1900, cl. May 16, 1900.

THEO. SEM.(Or. Con.) ANDOVER, MASS. Yr. beg. Sept. 20, '99. Ann. June 14, 1900.

BOSTON UNIVER. SCHOOL OF THEOL. (Methodist.) Year begins Sept. 20, '99.

NEW CHURCH THEOL. Sc., CAM-BRIDGE, MASS. (Swedenborg.) Yr. beg. Sept. 27, '99 ; ends June 20, 1900.

EPIS. THEO. SCHOOL AT CAMBRIDGE, MASS. Yr. beg. last Wed. in Sept.; ends 3d Wed in June.

NEWTON THEO. INST., NEWTON CEN-TRE, MASS. (Bapt.) Ann. Th. after 1st Sun. in June. Vac. fm. ann. to Wed. after 1st Sun. in Sept., fm. Chris. to New Year's.

DIVINITY SCH. OF HARVARD UNIV. Year same as that of Harvard Univ.

ST. JOHN'S ECCLESIASTICAL SEMI-NARY, Lake st., BRIGHTON, Mass. Beg. Sept. 12, '99, closes June 24, 1900.

TUFTS COLL. DIV. SCH. TUFTS COLL., MASS. (Univ.) Sch. yr. same as Coll.

BERKELEY DIV. SCH.(EPIS.),MIDDLE-TOWN, CT. Beg. Sept. 19. '99, ends June 6, 1900.

DIV. SCH. OF YALE UNIV., NEW HA-VEN, CONN. (Ortho. Cong.) Year beg. 4th Th. Sept.; closes 3d Wed. May.

HARTFORD THEOL. SEM., CONN. (Or-tho. Cong.) Acad. yr. from last Wed. Sept., to last Wed. in May.

Medical Schools.

MED. SCH. OF ME. BOWDOIN COLL., BRUNSWICK, ME. Beg. Dec. 28, '99, lasts 26w.

PORTLAND (ME.) SCH. FOR MED. INS. 2 terms ; beg. 1st Th. July and Oct.

MED. DEPT. DART. COLL., HANOVER, N.H. Comb. lecture and recitation tm. beg. July, 13, '99 ; ends last Tu. Feb. 1900. 1st course taken with Acad. course beg. Sept. 14, '99, 2w. vac. fm. Dec. 20, '99.

UNIV. OF VT., MED. DEP., BURLING-TON, VT. Beg. Jan. 4, ends June 28, 1900.

MASS. COLL. PHARMACY, BOSTON, MASS. Year beg. Sept. 25, '99.

MED. SCH. OF HARVARD UNIVER., BOSTON. Year same as that of Univer.

DENTAL SCH. HARV. UNI., BOSTON. Year same as that of Univer.

VETERINARY SCHOOL OF HARVARD UNIVER., Year same as that of Uni.

BOSTON DENTAL COLLEGE, BOSTON. Year begin 2d Mon in Sept.; ends 3d Wed. in June.

MED. SCH. OF TUFTS COLL., BOSTON, fr. last Wed. in Sept. to last Wed. May.

BOSTON UNIV. SCH. OF MED. (Homœ.) Open to both sexes. Beg. Oct. 5, '99.

COLLEGE OF PHYSICIANS AND SURGEONS, BOSTON. Year beg. 3d Tu. Sept.

MED. DEPART. OF YALE UNIV., NEW HAVEN, CT. 1st Th. Oct., till Com., with vac. same as that of Yale College.

Law Schools.

LAW SCH. OF HARVARD UNIV., CAMBRIDGE, MASS. Year same as Uni.

BOSTON UNIV. SCH. OF LAW. Beg. 1st Wed. Oct., ends 1st Wed. June.

YALE LAW SCH., N. HAVEN, CONN. Same as Yale University.

Scientific and Agric. Schools.

N.H. COLLEGE OF AGRIC. AND THE MECH. ARTS, DURHAM, N.H. Beg. Sept. 7, '99, Jan. 11, and Mar. 29, 1900.

THAYER, SCH. OF CIVIL ENGIN. HANOVER, N.H. Yr. fm. Aug. 1 to May 1.

UNIVER. OF VT., BURLINGTON, has courses in civil, mechanical, electrical, and sanitary engineering, and in agric.; also class. liter., sci. and chem.

MASS. AGRIC. COLLEGE, AMHERST, Mass. 3 terms. Terms beg. Sept. 7, '99, Jan. 3 and Apr. 4, 1900.

LAWRENCE SCIEN. SCHOOL (HARV. UNIV.), CAMBRIDGE, MASS. The year is the same as that of Harvard Univ.

THE BUSSEY INSTITUTION, JAMAICA PLAIN, MASS. (A sch. of Agric. & Hort. Harv. Univ.) Year same as Univ.

MASS. INST. OF TECHNOLOGY, BOSTON. Acad. year begins Sept. 27, '99. Degrees conferred June 5, 1900.

WORCESTER POLYTECH, INSTITUTE, WORC., MASS. Tms. fm. 2d Wed. Sept. to 3d Mon. Dec. and from 1st Tues. Jan. to to 4th Th. in Mar. and from 1st Th. in Apr. to last Th. but one in June.

R.I. COLL. OF AGRIC. AND MECH. ARTS, KINGSTOWN, R.I. 3 tms. 1st. beg. Sept. 20, '99. Com. June 17-19, 1900.

SHEFFIELD SCIENT. SCHOOL (YALE UNIV.), NEW HAVEN, CT. Terms same as those of Yale University.

CONN. AGRIC. COLL., STORRS, CONN. 4 tms. Beg. Sept. 18, '99, Jan. 2, 1900, Apr. 3, 1900, June 25, 1900. Com. June 21, 1900.

Normal Schools.

STATE NORMAL SCH., CASTINE, ME. Terms begin Aug. 29, '99, Dec. 12, '99, Mar. 13, 1900.

STATE NORMAL SCHOOL, GORHAM ME. 3 tms. Beg. Sept. 5, '99, Jan. 2, Apr. 3, 1900.

STATE NOR. SCH., FARMINGTON, ME. Tms. beg. Aug. 29, Dec. 12, '99, Mar. 20, Aug. 28, 1900.

STATE NORMAL SCH., PLYMOUTH, N.H. 2 tms. Beg. Feb. 6, Sept. 4, 1900.

STATE NOR. SCH., CASTLETON, VT. 40w.; year beg. Sept. 5, '99.

STATE NORMAL SCH., JOHNSON, VT. Tms. 20w. Beg. last Tu. Aug., 1st Tu. Feb.

STATE NORMAL SCH., RANDOLPH CENTER, VT. Year beg. 4th Tu. Aug.

NORMAL SCHOOLS OF MASSACHUSETTS. At Bridgewater, Fitchburg, Framingham, Hyannis, Lowell, North Adams, Salem, Westfield and Worcester. Yr. divided into 2 tms., 20w. ea. including recess of 1w. near mid. of trm. Vac. 2 or 3w. in winter, 9 or 10w. in sum. Exam. for adm. to all, Th. and Fri., June 28, 29, Tu. and Wed., Sept. 11 and 12, 1900.

MASS. NORMAL ART SCHOOL. 2 tms. Beg. Oct. 2, '99, and Feb. 19, 1900.

R.I. NORMAL SCHOOL, PROV., R.I. 2 tms. Spr. tm. beg. Feb. 5, closes June 29, 1900. Fall. tm. beg. Sept. 11, '99.

STATE NORMAL SCH., NEW BRITAIN, CONN. 1st tm. beg. Sept. 6, '99.

STATE NORMAL SCH., WILLIMANTIC, CONN. Yr. beg. 1st Tu. Sept.

MEETINGS OF FRIENDS IN NEW ENGLAND (1900).

The Yearly Meeting of Friends is held at Newport, R.I. Meeting on Ministry and Oversight, on 5th day, 6th m'th, 7th, at 9 a.m. For business, on 6th day, 8th, at 9 a.m. Public meetings for worship on First day. The Yearly Meeting is composed of the Quarterly Meetings of R. Island, Salem, Sandwich, Falmouth, Smithfield, Vassalboro', Dover, Fairfield, and Parsonsfield, held as follows:—

Rhode Island : 1st fifth day, 2d mo., at Providence, R.I.; 1st fifth day, 5th mo., at East Greenwich, R. I.; 1st fifth day, 8th mo., at Newport, R.I. and 1st fifth day, 11th mo., at Fall River, Mass.

Salem: 3d fifth day, 1st mo., at Boston, Mass.; 4th fifth day, 5th mo., at Amesbury, Mass; 3d fifth day, 8th mo., at Lynn, Mass.; 3d fifth day, 7th mo., at Weare, N.H.

Sandwich : 2d fifth day in 1st and 4th mos., at New Bedford, Mass.; 2d fifth day in 10th mo., at Sandwich, Mass.; 2d fifth day in 7th mo., at Falmouth, Mass.

Falmouth : On seventh day following the last sixth day in 1st mo. at Lewiston, Me.; 5th mo. at Deering, Me.; 8th mo. at Durham, Me.; 10th mo. at Windham, Me.

Smithfield : 2d fifth day, 2d mo., and 2d fifth day, 5th mo., at Worcester, Mass.; 2d fifth day, 8th mo., at Bolton, Mass.; 2d fifth day, 11th mo., at Woonsocket, R.I.

Vassalboro' : 2d sixth day, 2d and 11th mos., at East Vassalboro', Me.; last sixth day, 5th mo., at China, Me.; 2d sixth day, 9th mo., at Vassalboro', Me.

Dover : Seventh day aft. 1st fifth day, 1st mo., at Gonic, N.H.; seventh day aft. 3d fifth day, 4th mo., at Dover, N. H.; 8th mo. at N. Berwick, Me.; and 10th mo. at Rochester, N.H.

Fairfield : Seventh day aft. 1st sixth day, 2d mo., at Winthrop, Me.; seventh day before last sixth day, 5th mo., at Manchester, N.H.; seventh day aft. 1st sixth day, 9th mo., at St. Albans, Vt.; seventh day aft. 1st sixth day, 11th mo., at Fairfield, Me.

Parsonsfield : Seventh day aft. 1st sixth day, 9th mo., and seventh day after 2d fifth day, 1st mo., at East Parsonsfield, Me.; seventh day aft. 1st sixth day, 11th mo., and seventh after 3d fifth day, 5th mo., N. Sandwich, N.H.

COURTS OF THE UNITED STATES.

(Corrected Sept.. 1899. Congress may make changes).

The Supreme Court of the United States consists of one Chief and eight Associate Justices. Court comes in at Washington, D.C., on the 2d Monday in Oct. There are nine judicial circuits as follows : —

First Circuit. (Me., N. H., Mass., R. I.)
Second " (Vt., Conn., N. Y.)
Third " (Penn., N. J., Del.)
Fourth " (Md., Va., W. Va., N. C., S. C.)
Fifth " (Geo., Fla.. Ala., Miss., La., Tex,)
Sixth " (Ohio. Mich., Ky., Tenn.)
Seventh " (Ind., Ill., Wis.)
Eighth " (Minn., Ia., Mo., Kan., Ark., Neb., Colo., N. Dak., S. Dak., Wyoming, New Mexico, Oklahoma, Utah, Indian Territory.)
Ninth " (Cal., Oregon, Nev., Wash., Idaho, Montana, Arizona, Alaska.)

Circuit Court of Appeals, First and Second Circuits.

1st Circuit. (Maine, N.H., Mass., R.I.), at Boston, 1st Tu. in Oct. Sessions, 1st Tu. Oct., Jan., April.

2d Circuit. (Vt., Conn., N.Y.), at New York City, last Tu. in Oct.

Circuit Courts in First Circuit.

Maine, at Portland, Apr. 23 and Sept. 23.

New Hampshire, at Portsmouth, May 8; Concord, Oct. 8; Littleton, last Tu. Aug.

Massachusetts, at Boston, May 15 and Oct. 15.

Rhode Island, at Providence, June 15 and Nov. 15.

Circuit Courts in Second Circuit.

Vermont, at Windsor, 3d Tu. May; Rutland, 1st Tu. Oct.,; Burlington, 4th Tu. Feb.

Connecticut, at New Haven, 4th Tu. Apr.; Hartford 2d Tu. Oct.

Besides the above, Circuit Courts are held in the three New York districts in said circuit.

District Courts in First Circuit.

Maine, at Portland, 1st Tu. Feb. and Dec. ; Bath, 1st Tu. Sept. ; Bangor, 1st Tu. June.

New Hampshire, at Portsmouth, 3d Tu. Mar. and Sept.; Concord, 3d Tu. June and Dec.; Littleton, last Tu. Aug.

Massachusetts, at Boston, 3d Tu. Mar., 4th Tu. June, 2d Tu. Sept. and 1st Tu. Dec.

Rhode Island, at Newport, 2d Tu. May and 3d Tu. Oct.; Providence, 1st Tu. Feb. and Aug.

District Courts in Second Circuit.

Vermont, at Windsor, 3d Tu. May.; Rutland, 1st Tu. Oct.; Burlington, 4th Tu. Feb.

Connecticut, at Hartford, 4th Tu. May and 1st Tu. Dec.; New Haven, 4th Tu. Feb. and Aug.

In addition to the above there are three District Courts in New York in the second circuit.

U.S. REFEREES IN BANKRUPTCY IN NEW ENGLAND.

(Corrected Sept. 1899.)

Maine.

Androscoggin, Henry W. Oakes, Auburn.
Aroostook, Edwin L. Vail, Houlton.
Cumberland, Lewis Pierce, Portland.
Franklin, Joseph C. Holman, Farmington.
Hancock, John B. Redman, Ellsworth.
Kennebec, Fremont J. C. Little, Augusta.
Lincoln, Ozro D. Castner, Waldoboro.
Western District of Oxford, George A. Wilson, Paris.
Eastern District of Oxford, George D. Bisbee, Rumford Falls.
Penobscot, John R. Mason, Bangor.
Pisquataquis, John F. Sprague, Monson.
Sagadahoc, William T. Hall Jr., Bath.
Somerset, John W. Manson, Pittsfield.
Waldo, Hugh D. McLellan, Belfast.
Washington, Clement B. Donworth, Machias.
Northern District of York, John B. Donovan, Alfred.
Southern District of York, Walter L. Dane, Kennebunk.

New Hampshire.

1ST DISTRICT.—*Rockingham, Hillsbor-* ough, *Merrimack, Cheshire,* and *Sullivan* Counties, Lewis W. Clark, Manchester.
2D DISTRICT. — *Carroll, Belknap,* and *Strafford* Counties, Dwight Hall, Dover.
3D DISTRICT. — *Coös and Grafton* Counties, B. H. Corning, Littleton.

Vermont.

Addison, F. W. Tuttle, Vergennes.
Bennington, Geo. W. Hawkins, Bennington.
Caledonia, David E Porter, St. Johnsbury.
Chittenden, Geo. W. Deberville, Burlington.
Franklin, Hiram M. Mott, St. Albans.
Lamoille, F.H. McFarland, HydePark.
Orange, Roswell Farnham, Bradford.
Orleans, J. W. Redmond, Newport.
Rutland, Joel C. Baker, Rutland.
Washington, E. H. Deavitt, Montpelier.
Windham, Anthony E. Schwenk, Brattleboro.
Windsor, Gilbert A. Davis, Windsor.

Massachusetts.

Berkshire, Chas. E. Burke, Pittsfield.
Bristol, Wendell H. Cobb, New Bedford.
Essex, Wm. M. Thompson, Lawrence.

U. S. REFEREES IN BANKRUPTCY (Continued).

Massachusetts (continued).

Franklin, Henry J. Field, Greenfield.

Hampden, Chas. W. Bosworth, Springfield.

Hampshire, Arthur Watson, Northampton.

Middlesex, Forrest C. Manchester, Winchester.

Norfolk, Emery B. Gibbs, Brookline.

Plymouth, Chas. B. Barnes, Hingham.

Suffolk, Lewis G. Farmer and James M. Olmstead, Boston.

Worcester, Chas. F. Aldrich, Worcester.

Rhode Island.

Providence, Nathan W. Littlefield, Pawtucket.

Newport, Clark Burdick, Newport.

Connecticut.

Fairfield, Jno. W. Banks, Bridgep't.

Hartford, Francis H. Parker, Hartford.

Litchfield, Frank B. Munn, Winsted.

Middlesex, A. B. Calef, Middletown.

New Haven, H. G. Newton, N. Haven.

New London, A. A. Browning, Norwich.

Windham, Jno. F. Carpenter, Putnam.

COURTS IN THE STATE OF MAINE.
(Corrected September, 1899.)

Supreme Judicial Court.

LAW TERMS.

Portland, 3d Tu. July, for counties of Franklin, Oxford, Androscoggin, York, and Cumberland.

Augusta, 4th Tu. May, for counties of Somerset, Knox, Lincoln, Sagadahoc, and Kennebec.

Bangor, 3d Tu. June, for counties of Aroostook, Washington, Piscataquis, Hancock, Waldo, and Penobscot.

TRIAL TERMS.

Androscoggin Co., at Auburn, 3d Tu. Jan., Apr., and Sept.

Aroostook Co., *civil and crim.,* at Houlton, 3d Tu. Apr. and adjourns to Caribou; and 3d Tu. Sept.; *civil* at Caribou, 1st Tu. Dec.

Cumberland Co., *civil business*, at Portland, 2d Tu. Jan., Apr. and Oct.

Franklin Co., at Farmington, *civil*, 1st Tu. June; *civil and crim.*, 1st Tu. Feb. and 4th Tu. Sept.

Hancock Co., at Ellsworth, *civil*, 3d Tu. Jan.; *civ. and crim.*, 2d Tu. Apr., Oct.

Kennebec Co., *civil business*, at Augusta, 1st. Tu. Mar. and 3d Tu. Oct.

Knox Co., at Rockland, 2d Tu. Mar. and Dec. and 3d Tu. Sept.

Lincoln Co., at Wiscasset, *civil and crim.*, 4th Tu. Apr. and Oct.

Oxford Co., at Paris, *civil*, 1st Tu. May; *civil and crim.*, 2d Tu. Feb. and Oct.

Penobscot Co., at Bangor, *civil business*, 1st Tu. Jan., Apr. and Oct.; *crim.* 1st Tu. Feb. and 2d Tu. Aug.

Piscataquis Co., at Dover, *civil and crim.*, last Tu. Feb. and 3d Tu. Sept.

Sagadahoc Co., at Bath, 1st Tu. Apr. and 3d Tu. Aug. and Dec.

Somerset Co., at Skowhegan, *civil and crim.*, 3d Tu. Mar., Sept. and Dec.

Waldo Co., at Belfast, 1st Tu. Jan. and 3d Tu. Apr. and Sept.

Washington Co., at Machias, 2d Tu. Jan. and Oct.; Calais, 4th Tu. Apr.

York Co., at Saco, 1st. Tu. Jan.; Alfred, 3d Tu. May and Sept.

Superior Court for Cumberl'd Co.

At Portland, *civil* only, 1st Tu. Feb. Mar., Apr., Oct., Nov., Dec.; *civil and crim.*, 1st Tu. Jan., May and Sept.

Superior Court for Kennebec Co.

At Augusta, *civil and crim*, 1st Tu. Apr., Sept. and Dec. At Waterville, *civil*, 1st Tu. Feb., 2d Tu. June and Nov.

COUNTY COMMISSIONERS' SESSIONS IN MAINE.
(Corrected September, 1899.)

Androscoggin, at Auburn, 1st Tu. Apr. and Oct.

Aroostook, at Houlton, 1st Tu. Jan. and July.

Cumberland, at Portland, terms of record, 1st Tu. Jan. and June; and regular sessions, 1st. Tu. each month.

Franklin, at Farmington, last Tu. Apr. and Dec.

Hancock, at Ellsworth, 3d Tu. Jan. and 2d Tu. Apr. and Oct.

Kennebec, at Augusta, 3d Tu. Apr., Aug. and Dec.

Knox, at Rockland, 1st Tu, Apr. and Dec. and 3d Tu. Aug.

Lincoln, at Wiscasset, 2d Tu. May, 1st Tu Sept. and last Mon. Dec.

Oxford, at Paris, 2d Tu. May, 1st Tu. Sept. and last Tu. Dec.

Penobscot, at Bangor, 1st Tu. Jan., Apr., July and Oct.

Piscataquis, at Dover, 1st Tu. Apr., Aug. and Dec.

Sagadahoc, at Bath, 1st Tu. Mar., July and Nov.

Somerset, at Skowhegan, 2d Tu. Mar., Aug. and Dec.

Waldo, at Belfast, 2d Tu. Apr., 3d Tu. Aug. and Dec.

Washington, at Machias, 1st Tu. Jan. and Oct. ; at Calais, 4th Tu. Apr.

York, tms. of rec., 1st Tu. Apr. and Oct.; reg. sessions 1st Tu. each mo., at the place where Probate Court is held.

PROBATE COURTS IN MAINE.
(Corrected September, 1899.)

Androscoggin, at Auburn, 2d Tu. each mo.

Aroostook, at Houlton, 3d Tu. Jan., Mar., May, July, Sept., and Nov.; Caribou, 3d Tu. Feb., Apr., June, Aug., Oct., and Dec.; Fort Kent, last Tu. June.

Cumberland, at Portland, 1st and 3d Tu. each mo. except Aug.

PROBATE COURTS IN MAINE (Continued).

Franklin, at Farmington, 1st Tu. each mo.

Hancock, at Ellsworth, 1st Tu. Jan., Mar., Apr., June, Aug., Oct. and Nov.; Bucksport, 1st Tu. Feb., May and Dec.; Bluehill, 1st Tu. July and Sept.

Kennebec, at Augusta, 2d and 4th Mon. each mo. except Sept., and 4th Mon. Sept.

Knox, at Rockland, 3d Tu. each mo.

Lincoln, at Wiscasset, 1st Tu. each mo. except Aug.

Oxford, at So. Paris, 3d Tu. each mo.; Fryeburg, 1st Tu. June and Dec.

Penobscot, at Bangor, last Tu. ea mo.

Piscataquis, at Dover, 1st Tu. each mo.

Sagadahoc, at Bath, 1st and 2d Tu. each mo.

Somerset, at Skowhegan, 2d Tu. each mo.

Waldo, at Belfast, 2d Tu. each mo.

Washington, at Calais, 2d Tu. June; Cherryfield, 2d Tu. Sept.; Eastport, 2d Tu. July; Machias, 2d Tu. Feb., Apr., Nov. and Dec.

York, at Alfred, 1st Tu. Apr., May, June, Aug., Sept., Oct., Nov. and Dec.; Biddeford, 1st Tu. Mar. and July; Saco, 1st Tu. Jan. and Feb.

COURTS IN THE STATE OF NEW HAMPSHIRE.

(Corrected September, 1899.)

Supreme Court.
LAW TERMS.

Two terms are held each year, 1st Tu. June and Dec., both at Concord. Adjourned terms, March and July.

TRIAL TERMS.

Belknap Co., at Laconia, 1st Tu. May and Nov.

Carroll Co., at Ossipee, 3d Tu. Apr. and Oct.

Cheshire Co., at Keene, 1st Tu. Apr. and 3d Tu. Oct.

Coös Co., at Colebrook, 1st Tu. Feb. and Sept.; Lancaster, 3d Tu. Apr. and Oct.

Grafton Co., at Lebanon, 3d Tu. Jan., Apr., July and Oct.; Plymouth, 2d Tu. Feb., May, Aug. and Nov.; Woodsville, 3d Tu. Mar., June, Sept. and Dec.; Canaan, 1st Tu. June and Dec.; Haverhill, 1st Tu. Feb., May and Nov.

Hillsborough Co., at Manchester, 1st Tu. Jan. and May; Nashua, 3d Tu. Sept.

Merrimack Co., at Concord, 1st Tu. Apr. and Oct.

Rockingham Co., at Portsmouth, 3d Tu. Oct.; Exeter, 3d Tu. Jan. and 2d Tu. Apr.

Strafford Co., at Dover, 2d Tu. Feb. and 1st Tu. Sept.

Sullivan Co., at Newport, 1st Tu. May and Nov.

Probate Courts.

[*If the term of a probate court falls on a legal holiday, said court is held on the next secular day thereafter.*]

Belknap Co., at Laconia, 3d Tu. of each month.

Carroll Co., at Conway, 1st, Tu. Jan., May and Sept.; W. Ossipee, 1st Tu. Feb., June and Oct.; Ossipee Corner, 1st Tu. Mar., July and Nov.; Sanbornville, 1st Tu. Apr., Aug. and Dec.

Cheshire Co. at Keene, 1st and 3d Fri. Jan., Feb., Mar., Apr., May, June, Sept., Oct., Nov. and Dec.; 1st Fri. July and 3d Fri. Aug.

Coös Co., at Colebrook, 4th Tu. Jan. and Aug.; Lancaster, 1st Tu. Jan., Mar., May, July and Nov.; Gorham, 1st Tu. Apr. and Oct.; Berlin 3d Tu. Jan. and June.

Grafton Co., at Lisbon, 3d Tu. Apr. and Oct.; Plymouth, 2d Tu. May and Nov.; Canaan, 1st Tu. June and Dec.; Woodsville, 3d Tu. Mar. and Sept.; Haverhill, 1st Tu. July; Bristol, 3d Tu. July; Littleton, 3d Tu. Jan.; Wentworth, 3d Tu. Aug.; Orford, 3d Tu. Feb.; Lebanon, 1st Tu. Mar. and Sept.

Hillsborough Co., at Manchester, 3d Tu. of each month; Nashua, 4th Tu. Feb., Apr., June, Aug., Oct., and Dec.; Francestown, Fri. aft. 4th Tu. Aug.; Amherst, Fri. aft. 4th Tu. June and Dec.; Peterborough, Fri. aft. 4th Tu. Feb., May and Nov.; Greenville, Fri. aft. 4th. Tu. Apr. and Oct.; Hillsborough Bridge, Fri. aft. 4th Tu. Jan. and July; Milford, Fri. aft. 4th Tu. Mar. and Sept.

Merrimack Co., at Concord, 2d and 4th Tu. each month.

Rockingham Co., at Exeter, Wed. aft. 3d Tu. July, and Wed. aft. 1st Tu. of each other month except Aug.; Portsmouth, 1st Tu. Jan., Mar., May, July, Sept. and Nov.; Derry, 1st Tu. Feb., June and Oct., and 4th Tu. Dec.; Raymond, 1st Tu. Apr. and Dec. and 3d Tu. July; Hampton, 4th Tu. Feb. and July.

Strafford Co., at Dover, 1st Tu. each month; Farmington, 3d Tu. Apr., Aug. and Dec.; Rochester, 3d Tu. Jan., Mar., Feb., May, July, Sept. and Nov.; Somersworth, 3d Tu. June and Oct.;

Sullivan Co., at Newport, last Wed. Feb., Apr., June, Aug., Oct. and Dec.; Claremont, last Wed. Jan., Mar., May, July, Sept. and Nov.

COURTS IN THE STATE OF VERMONT.

(Corrected Sept. 1899. Legislature meets in October, 1900, and may make changes.)

Supreme Court.

Three general terms for all counties at Montpelier, 4th Tu. Jan., Oct., 2d Tu. May; and special terms may be held at such other times as the judges may appoint.

County Courts.

Addison Co., at Middlebury, 1st Tu. June and Dec.

Bennington Co., at Manchester, 1st Tu. June; Bennington, 1st Tu. Dec.

Caledonia Co., at St. Johnsbury, 1st Tu. June and Dec.

COURTS IN THE STATE OF VERMONT (Continued).

Chittenden Co., at Burlington, 1st Wed. aft. 1st Tu. Mar. and Sept.

Essex Co., at Guildhall, 1st Wed. aft. 1st Tu. Mar. and Sept.

Franklin Co., at St. Albans, 1st Wed. aft. 1st Tu. Mar. and Sept.

Grand Isle Co., at North Hero, 2d Tu. Jan. and Aug.

Lamoille Co., at Hyde Park, 1st Tu. June and Dec.

Orange Co., at Chelsea, 1st Tu. June and Dec.

Orleans Co., at Newport, 1st Wed. aft. 1st Tu. Mar. and Sept.

Rutland Co., at Rutland, 1st Wed. aft. 1st Tu. Mar. and Sept.

Washington Co., at Montpelier 1st Wed. aft. 1st Tu. Mar. and Sept.

Windham Co., at Newfane, 1st Wed. aft. 1st Tu. Mar. and Sept.

Windsor Co., at Woodstock, 1st Tu. June and Dec

Probate Courts. — A Probate Court is held in each Probate District at least once in each month, at times and places appointed by the respective judges. Said courts are open at all times for the transaction of certain business.

COURTS IN THE STATE OF MASSACHUSETTS.

(Corrected September, 1899. Legislature meets in Jan. 1900, and may make changes,)

Supreme Judicial Court.

LAW SITTINGS.

A law sitting for the Commonwealth is held at Boston on the 1st Wed. of Jan. of each year, which may be adjourned to places and times most conducive to the interests of the public, and at which are entered and determined questions of law arising in the counties of Barnstable, Middlesex, Norfolk, and Suffolk, and also in other counties where special provisions are not made therefor. And law sittings of said court are also held annually as follows : —

Berkshire Co., at Pittsfield, 2d Tu. Sept.

Bristol, Nantucket, and Dukes Cos., at Taunton, 4th Mo. Oct.

Essex Co., at Salem, 1st Tu. Nov.

Hampden Co., at Springfield, 2d Mo. after 2d Tu. Sept.

Hampshire and Franklin Cos., at Northampton and Greenfield, Monday after 2d Tu. Sept. At Northampton in even years. [Oct.

Plymouth Co., at Plymouth, 3d Tu.

Worcester Co., at Worcester, 3d Mo. after 2d Tu. Sept.

JURY SITTINGS.

Barnstable Co., at Barnstable, 1st Tu. May. [May.

Berkshire Co., at Pittsfield, 2d Tu.

Bristol, Nantucket, and Dukes Cos., at New Bedford, 2d Tu. Nov.; Taunton, 3d Tu. Apr.

Essex Co., at Salem, 3d Tu. Apr., and 1st Tu. Nov. [Apr.

Franklin Co., at Greenfield, 2d Tu.

Hampden Co., at Springfield, 4th Tu. Apr.

Hampshire Co., at Northampton, 3d Tu. Apr.

Middlesex Co., at Lowell, 3d Tu. Apr.; East Cambridge, 3d Tu. Oct.

Norfolk Co., at Dedham, 3d Tu. Feb.

Plymouth Co., at Plymouth, 2d Tu. May.

Suffolk Co., at Boston, 2d Tu. Sept., and 1st Tu. Apr. [Apr.

Worcester Co., at Worcester, 2d Tu.

Superior Court.

Barnstable Co., at Barnstable, 1st Tu. Apr., 2d Tu. Oct.

Berkshire Co., at Pittsfield, (civil) 4th Mo. Feb., June and Oct.; (crim.) 2d Mo. Jan. and July.

Bristol Co., (civil) at Taunton, 1st Mo. Mar. and 2d Mo. Sept.; New Bedford, 1st Mo. May and Dec.; (crim.) Taunton, 1st Mo. Feb.; Fall River, 1st Mon. Nov.; New Bedford, 1st Mo. June. Either crim. term may be adjourned to Fall River. [April and Sept.

Dukes Co., at Edgartown, last Tu.

Essex Co., (civil) at Salem, 1st Mo. June and Dec.; Lawrence, 1st Mo. Mar.; Newburyport, 1st Mo. Oct.; (crim.) Salem, 2d Mo. Jan.; Newburyport, 2d Mo. May; Lawrence, 2d Mo. Sept.

Franklin Co., at Greenfield, 2d Mo. Mar., July and Nov.

Hampden Co., at Springfield, (civil) 1st Mo. Jan., 2d Mo. Mar. and June, and 4th Mo Oct.; (crim.) 1st Mo. May, 4th Mo. Sept. and 3d Mo. Dec.

Hampshire Co., at Northampton, (civil) 3d Mo. Feb., 1st Mo. June and 3d Mo. Oct.; (crim.) 2d Mo. June and 3d Mo. Dec.

Middlesex Co., (civil) at Lowell, 2d Mo. June and 2d. Mo. Dec.; (crim.) Cambridge, 2d Mo. Feb. and 1st Mo. June; Lowell, 3d Mo. Oct.

Nantucket Co., at Nantucket, 1st Tu. July and Oct.

Norfolk Co., at Dedham, (civil) 1st Mo. Jan., May and Oct.; (crim.) 1st Mo. Apr., Sept. and Dec.

Plymouth Co., at Plymouth, 2d Mo. Feb. and June and 4th Mo. Oct.; Brockton, 1st Mon. May and Dec.

Suffolk Co., at Boston, (civil) 1st Tu. Jan., April, July and Oct.; (crim.) 1st Mo. each month. The superior court holds, each mo., except in July, Aug. and Sept., a session for the speedy trial of certain causes.

Worcester Co., (civil) at Worcester, 1st Mo. Mar. and 2d Mo. Dec.; Fitchburg, 2d Mo. June and Nov.; (crim.) at Worcester, 3d Mo. Jan., 2d Mo. May and 3d Mo. Oct.; Fitchburg, 3d Mo. Aug.

MUNICIPAL AND POLICE COURTS.

(Corrected September, 1899.)

Saturday of each week is the return day for writs in civil actions.

Municipal Courts.
Boston, civil and crim., daily, 9.30 a.m.

Brighton District, crim. daily, 9 a.m.; civil, Wed.

MUNICIPAL AND POLICE COURTS, MASS. (Continued).

Brookline, *crim.,* daily, 9 a.m.; *civil,* Tu.

Charlestown District, *crim.,* daily, 9 a.m.; *civil,* Th.

Dorchester District, *crim.,* daily, 9 a.m.; *civil ,* Sat., 9.30 a.m.

Roxbury District, *crim.,* daily, 9.30 a.m.; *civil* Tu. 10 a.m.

So. Boston District, *crim.,* daily, 9 a.m.; *civil,* Tu. 11 a.m.

W. Roxbury District *crim.,* daily, 9 a.m.; *civil,* Mon. 2 p.m.

Police Courts.

Brockton, for Brockton, Bridgewater, East and West Bridgewater, *crim.,* daily, 8.15 a.m.; *civil,* Sat. 9. a.m.

Chelsea, for Chelsea and Revere, *crim.,* daily, 9 a.m.; *civil,* Tu. 10 a.m.

Chicopee, *crim.,* daily, 9 a.m.; *civil,* Sat. 10 a.m.

Fitchburg, *crim.,* daily, 9. a.m.; *civil,* Th. 10 a.m.

Gloucester, for Gloucester, Rockport, Manchester and Essex, *crim.,* daily, 9 a.m.; *civil,* Sat. 10 a.m.

Holyoke, *crim.,* daily, 9 a.m.; *civil,* Sat.

Lawrence, *crim.,* daily, 9 a.m.; *civil,* 2d and 4th Tu. 10 a.m.

Lee, *crim.,* daily, 9 a.m.; *civil,* Fri.

Lowell, *crim.,* daily, 10 a.m.; *civil,* any day assigned by the court on the preceding Wed.

Lynn, *crim.,* daily, 10 a.m.; *civil,* any day assigned by the court on the preceding Sat.

Marlborough, *crim.,* daily, 3 p.m.; *civil,* Sat. 9 a.m.

Newburyport for Newburyport and Newbury, *crim.,* daily, 10 a.m.; *civil,* 1st and 3d Wed. each month.

Newton, *crim.,* daily; *civil,* Tu. 8.30 a.m.

Somerville, *crim.,* daily, 9 a.m.; *civil,* Sat.

Springfield, for Springfield, Agawam, Longmeadow, Hampden, W. Springfield and Wilbraham, *crim.,* daily, 9 a.m.; *civil,* Sat., 10 a.m. [*civil,* sat.

Williamstown, *crim.,* daily, 9 a.m.;

DISTRICT COURTS.

(Corrected September, 1899. Legislature meets in January, 1900, and may make changes,)

Saturday of each week is return day for writs in civil actions.

1st of Barnstable. For Barnstable, Yarmouth, Sandwich, Bourne, Falmouth and Mashpee. At Bourne, *civil and crim.,* Sat. at 9 a.m.; Barnstable, *crim.,* daily (except Sat.); *civil,* Mon., 9 a.m.

2d of Barnstable. For Provincetown, Truro, Wellfleet, Eastham, Orleans, Brewster, Chatham, Harwich and Dennis. At Harwich, *civil and crim.,* Fri. 9 a.m. ; Provincetown, *crim.,* daily (except Fri.), at 1 p.m., *civil,* Th.

No. Berkshire. For No. Adams, Clarksburg and Florida, at No. Adams, *crim.,* daily, 9 a.m.; *civil,* Wed.

Central Berkshire. For Pittsfield, Dalton, Hancock, Hinsdale, Lanesborough, Peru, Richmond and Washington, at Pittsfield, *crim.,* daily, 10 a.m.; *civil,* Sat.

So. Berkshire. For Alford, Egremont, Great Barrington, Monterey, Mt. Washington, New Marlboro and Sheffield, at Great Barrington, *crim.,* daily; *civil,* Sat. at 10 a.m.

4th of Berkshire. For Adams, Cheshire, Savoy and Windsor, at Adams, *crim.,* daily; *civil,* Sat. 9. a.m.

1st of Bristol. For Taunton, Rehoboth, Berkley, Dighton, Seekonk, Attleborough, North Attleborough, Norton, Mansfield, Easton and Raynham, at Taunton and Attleborough, *crim.,* daily, 9 a.m.; *civil,* Mon. at Taunton, 10 a.m.

2d of Bristol. For Fall River, Freetown, Somerset and Swansea, at Fall River, *crim.,* daily, 10 a.m.; *civil,* Mon.

[2d and 3d Dist. Courts of Bristol have concurrent jurisdiction in Westport and Freetown.]

3d of Bristol. For New Bedford, Fair Haven, Acushnet, Dartmouth and

Westport, at New Bedford, *crim.,* daily; *civil,* Mon. and Th. 10 a.m.

Dukes. For Edgartown, Cottage City, Tisbury, West Tisbury, Chilmark, Gay Head and Gosnold, *civil and crim.,* at Cottage City, on each alternate Sat., and at Edgartown and Tisbury alternately in the intervening weeks, 10 a.m.

Central of Northern Essex. For Haverhill, Boxford, Bradford, Georgetown and Groveland, at Haverhill, *crim.,* daily; *civil,* 1st and 3d Wed. each month, 9 a.m.

East Boston. For Wards one and two of Boston and Winthrop, *crim.,* daily; *civil,* Mon. 10 a.m.

1st of Essex. For Salem, Beverly, Danvers, Hamilton, Middleton, Topsfield, and Wenham, at Salem, *crim.,* daily, 9 a.m.; *civil,* Wed. 10 a.m.

2d of Essex. For Amesbury and Merrimac at Amesbury, *crim.,* daily; *civil,* 2d and 4th Wed. 9 a.m.

Franklin. For Greenfield, Turner's Falls, Shelburne Falls and Buckland, *crim.,* daily, at either or any of these, as public convenience may require; *civil,* at Greenfield, 1st Sat. each mo. 9 a.m.; Shelburne Falls, 3d Sat. each mo. ; Turner's Falls, 4th Sat. each month.

E. Franklin. For Orange, Erving, Warwick and New Salem. at Orange, *crim.,* daily; *civil,* Sat. 9 a.m.

E. Hampden. For Palmer, Brimfield, Monson, Holland and Wales, at Palmer, *crim.,* daily; *civil,* Sat. 9 a.m.

W. Hampden. For Westfield, Chester, Granville, Southwick, Russell, Blandford, Tolland and Montgomery, at Westfield, *crim.,* daily; *civil,* Sat., 9 a.m.

Hampshire. At Northampton, *crim.,* daily, exc. 1st and 3d Wed. and 2d and 4th Fri. 9 a.m.; *civil,* Mon. 10 a.m.; Amherst, *crim. and civil,* 1st and 3d

DISTRICT COURTS, MASS. (Continued).

Wed.; Huntington, 2d and 4th Th.; Ware, Fri., 9 a.m.; Belchertown, Easthampton and Cummington at option of judge.

1st of N. Middlesex. For Ayer, Groton, Pepperell, Townsend, Ashby, Shirley, Westford, Littleton and Boxborough, at Ayer, *crim.*, daily; *civil*, last Sat. of each month, 9 a.m.

Central Middlesex. For Acton, Bedford, Carlisle, Concord, Lincoln, Maynard, Stow and Lexington, at Concord, *crim.*, daily; *civil*, 1st and 3d Wed. each month, 9 a.m.

1st of E. Middlesex. For No. Reading, Wakefield, Melrose, Malden, Everett and Medford, at Malden, *crim.*, daily; *civil*, Mon. 9 a.m.

2d of E. Middlesex. For Watertown, Weston and Waltham, at Waltham, *crim.*, daily 9 a.m.; *civil*, Sat. 9.30 a.m.

3d of E. Middlesex. For Cambridge, Arlington and Belmont, at Cambridge, *crim.*, daily 9 a.m.; *civil*, Th. 10 a.m.

4th of E. Middlesex. For Woburn, Winchester, Burlington, Wilmington, Reading and Stoneham, at Woburn, *crim.*, daily; *civil*, Sat. 9 a.m.

1st of S. Middlesex. For Ashland, Framingham, Holliston, Sherborn, Sudbury and Wayland, at S. Framingham, *crim.*, daily; *civil*, Mon., 9.30 a.m.

E. Norfolk. For Randolph, Braintree, Cohasset, Weymouth, Quincy, Holbrook and Milton, at Quincy, *crim.*, daily; *civil*, Tu. 9. a.m.

N. Norfolk. For Dedham, Hyde Park, Dover, Norwood, Westwood, Medfield, Needham and Wellesley, at Dedham, *crim.*, daily; *civil*, Tu. 9 a.m.

S. Norfolk. For Stoughton, Canton, Avon and Sharon, at Stoughton; *crim.*, daily; *civil*, Tu. 9 a.m.

W. Norfolk. For Bellingham, Foxboro, Franklin, Medway, Millis, Norfolk, Walpole and Wrentham *crim.*, at Walpole, Mon., Wed. and Fri. 8.30 a.m. Franklin, Tu., Thurs. and Sat. 9 a.m.; *civil*, at Walpole on Wed., and at Franklin, Sat., 9 a.m.

2d of Plymouth. For Abington, Whitman, Rockland, Hingham, Hull, Hanover, Scituate, Norwell and Hanson, *civil and crim.*, at Abington, Mon.,

Wed., Th., Sat. 9 a.m.; Hingham, Tu. and Fri. 9 a.m.

3d of Plymouth. For Plymouth, Kingston, Plympton, Pembroke, Duxbury and Marshfield, at Plymouth, *crim.*, daily; *civil*, any court day, 9 a.m.

4th of Plymouth. For Middleborough, Wareham, Lakeville, Marion, Mattapoisett and Rochester, *crim.*, at Middleborough, Tu., Wed., and Sat.; Wareham, Mon. Th., and Fri.; *civil*, at Middleborough, Sat., 8 a.m. in summer and 9 a.m. in winter.

[3d and 4th Districts have concurrent jurisdiction in Carver.]

1st of N. Worcester. For Athol, Petersham, Phillipston, Royalston, Templeton, Gardner and Hubbardston, *crim.*, at Gardner and Athol as public convenience may require; *civil*, writs, etc., ret'd at Gardner; trials at Gardner 1st and 3d Sat. each month, 9 a.m.; Athol, 2d and 4th Sat. each month, 10 a.m.

1st of S. Worcester. For Sturbridge, Southbridge, Charlton, Dudley, Oxford and Webster, *crim.*, at Southbridge, Mo., Wed., and Fri.; Webster, Tu., Th. and Sat., 9 a.m.; *civil*, at Southbridge, Mo., Webster, Sat., 9.30 a.m.

2d of S. Worcester. For Blackstone, Uxbridge, Douglas and Northbridge, *crim.*, at Blackstone, Mon., Wed. and Fri. at Uxbridge, Tu., Th., and Sat.; *civil* at Uxbridge, Sat., 9 a.m.

3d of S. Worcester. For Milford, Hopedale, Mendon and Upton, at Milford, *crim.*, daily; *civil*, Sat. 9 a.m.

Central Worcester. For Worcester, Millbury, Sutton, Auburn, Leicester, Paxton, W. Boylston, Holden and Shrewsbury, at Worcester, *crim.*, daily. 9 a.m.; *civil*, Sat. 9.30 a.m.; for July and Aug. Fri. 9.30 a.m.

1st of E. Worcester. For Southborough, Westborough, and Grafton, *crim.*, at Westborough, Mo., Wed., Fri. and Sat.; Grafton, Tues. and Th.; *civil*, at Westborough, regularly Mon. and any day by agreement, 9 a.m.

2d of E. Worcester. For Northborough, Clinton, Berlin, Bolton, Boylston, Harvard, Lancaster and Sterling, at Clinton, *crim.*, daily; *civil*, 2d and 4th Sat. each month 9 a.m.

PROBATE COURTS.

(Corrected September, 1899. Legislature meets in January, 1900, and may make changes.)

When the appointed day falls on a holiday, or day of national or state election, the court is held on the next secular day thereafter.

Barnstable. At Barnstable, 2d Tu. Jan., Feb., Mar., May, June, July, Aug., Sept., Nov., Dec. and 1st Tu. Apr. and Oct.

Berkshire. At Pittsfield, 1st Tu. Jan., Feb., Mar., Apr., May, June, Sept., Oct. and Dec., 3d Tu. July, and Wed. aft. 1st Mo. Nov.; Lee, Wed. aft. 1st Tu. in Jan. Apr. and Oct., and Wed. after 3d Tu. July; Adams, Th. after 1st Tu. Jan. and Oct., Wed. after 1st Tu. Mar.,

and Th. after 3d Tu. July; Gt. Barrington, Wed. after 1st Tu. Feb., May, Sept. and Dec.

Bristol. At Taunton, 1st Fri. Mar., June, Sept. and Dec., 3d Fri. Jan., Apr., Oct. and Dec.; New Bedford, 1st Fri., Feb., May, Aug. and Nov., 3d Fri. Mar., June and Sept.; Fall River, 1st Fri. Jan., Apr., July and Oct., 3d Fri. Feb., May and Nov., 2d Fri. Sept.

Dukes Co. At Holmes' Hole village, 3d Mo. Apr. and 1st Mo. Sept.; Edgartown, 3d Mo. Jan. and July, and 1st Mo. Mar. and Dec.; W. Tisbury, 1st Mo. June and 3d Mo. Oct.

PROBATE COURTS, MASS. (Continued).

Essex. At Salem, 1st Mo. each mo., and 3d Mo. each mo. except Aug.; Lawrence, 2d Mo. Jan., Mar., May, June, July, Sept. and Nov.; Haverhill, 2d Mo. Apr. and Oct. Newburyport, 4th Mo. Jan., Mar., May, June, July, Sept., Nov.; Gloucester, 4th Mo. Apr. and Oct.

Franklin. At Greenfield, 1st Tu. each month exept Nov., 2d Tu. Jan., Apr. and Nov., 4th Tu. each month except Aug.; Northfield, 3d Tu. May and Sept.; Orange, 2d Tu. Mar., June, Sept. and Dec., 3d Tu. June and 4th Tu. Sept.; Conway; 3d Tu. June; Shelburne Falls, 2d Tu. Feb., May and Oct.

Hampden. At Springfield, 1st Wed. each month except Aug.; Holyoke, 3d Wed. Jan., Mar., June and Oct.; Palmer, 2d Wed. Feb., May and Sept., and 4th Wed. Nov.; at Westfield, 3d Wed. Feb., May, Sept. and Dec.

Hampshire. At Northampton, 1st Tu. each month; Amherst, 2d Tu. Jan., Mar., June, Aug. and Nov.; Belcher-town, 2d Tu. May and Oct.; Williams-burg, 3d Tu. May and Oct.; Ware, 2d Tu. Feb., 3d Tu. June and 2d Tu. Sept. and Dec.

Middlesex. At Cambridge (East), 1st, 2d and 4th Tu. each month; Lowell, 3d Tu. each month except Aug.

Nantucket. At Nantucket, on Th. after 2d Tu. each month.

Norfolk. At Dedham, 1st and 3d Wed., Quincy, 2d Wed., Brookline, 4th Wed. each month except Aug.

Plymouth. At Plymouth, 2d Mo. each month except Aug.; Brockton, 4th Mo. each month except July.

Suffolk. At Boston, each Th. in the year except 1st, 2d, 4th and 5th Th. Aug.

Worcester. At Worcester, 1st, 2d, 3d and 5th, Tu. each month except Aug.; Fitchburg, 4th Tu. each month except Aug.; Milford, 2d Tu. Apr. and Sept.; Templeton, 2d Tu. May and Oct.; Barre, Wed. after 2d Tu. May and Oct.

REGISTERS OF PROBATE.

Barnstable, F. H. Lothrop, Barnstable.
Berkshire, Fred R. Shaw, Pittsfield.
Bristol, Arthur M. Alger, Taunton.
Dukes, Beriah T. Hillman, Edgartown.
Essex, Jeremiah T. Mahoney, Salem.
Franklin, F. M. Thompson, Greenfield.
Hampden, S. B. Spooner, Springfield.

Hampshire, H. M. Abbott, N'hampton.
Middlesex, S. H. Folsom, East Camb.
Nantucket, Henry Riddell, Nantucket.
Norfolk, Jonathan Cobb, Dedham.
Plymouth, John C. Sullivan, Plymouth.
Suffolk, Elijah George, Boston.
Worcester, G. H. Harlow, Worcester.·

COURT OF REGISTRATION.
LAND TITLES.

At BOSTON, open for business, daily except Sundays and legal holidays. Sittings may be held in any city or town at the discretion of the court.

COUNTY COMMISSIONERS' MEETINGS IN MASSACHUSETTS.

(Corrected September, 1899.   Legislature meets in January, 1900, and may make changes.)

Barnstable, at Barnstable, 2d Tu. of Apr. and Oct.

Berkshire, at Pittsfield, 1st Tu. Jan., Apr., July and Oct.

Bristol, at Taunton, 4th Tu. Mar. and Sept.

Dukes, at Edgartown, Wed. aft. 3d Mo. May, and Wed. aft. 2d Mo. Nov.

Essex, at Ipswich, 2d Tu. Apr.; Salem, 2d Tu. July; Newburyport, 2d Tu. Oct.; Lawrence, last Tu. Aug.; and 4th Tu. Dec., at Ipswich, Salem or Newburyport, as they shall order at their next preceding meeting.

Franklin, at Greenfield, 1st Tu. Mar. and Sept., and 2d Tu. June and Dec.

Hampden, at Springfield, 2d Tu.

Apr., 1st Tu. Oct., and 4th Tu. June and Dec.

Hampshire, at Northampton, 1st Tu. of each month except June, and Tu. aft. 2d Mon. of June.

Middlesex, at Cambridge, 1st Tu. Jan. and 1st Tu. June; Lowell, 1st Tu. Sept.

Nantucket, 1st Wed. each month.

Norfolk, at Dedham, 3d Tu. Apr., 4th Tu. June and Sept., and last Wed. Dec.

Plymouth, at Plymouth, 1st Tu. Jan., 3d Tu. Mar. and 1st Tu. Aug.

Worcester, at Worcester, every Tu.; Fitchburg, last Wed. in each month.

COURTS IN THE STATE OF RHODE ISLAND.

(Corrected Sept., 1899.   Legislature meets in Jan. and May, 1900, and may make changes.)

Supreme Court.
APPELLATE DIVISION.

Newport Co., at Newport, 2d Mon. May, and 3d Mon. Sept.

Providence Co., at Providence, 4th Mon. Apr., May and Nov., 1st Mon. Oct.

Washington Co., at South Kingstown, 2d Mon. Apr. and Nov.

COMMON PLEAS DIVISION,

Bristol Co., at Bristol, 3d Mon. Feb.

and Sept.; 2d Mon. May, and 1st Mon. Dec.

Kent Co., at E. Greenwich, 2d Mon. Mar.; 4th Mon. May; 1st Mon. Oct.; 3d Mon. Dec.

Newport Co., at Newport, 3d Mon. Jan.; 2d Mon. Apr.; 4th Mon. June; 1st Mon. Nov.

Providence Co., at Providence, 3d Mon. Sept., and thence continuously to 3d Mon. July following, with adjourned session at Woonsocket.

COURTS IN STATE OF RHODE ISLAND (Continued).

Washington Co., at South Kingstown, 1st Mon. Jan., 4th Mon. Mar, 2d Mon. June and 3d Mon. Oct.; with adjourned session at Westerly.

District Courts.

Every District Court is open at all times for the transaction of *criminal business*.

1st Judicial District (Newport Co.), *civil*, at Newport each Tu. and Fri.; Tiverton 3d Th. each month.

2d District (South Kingstown, N'th Kingstown, Exeter and District of Narragansett), *civil*, at South Kingstown each Mon.; North Kingstown each Th.; Exeter 3d Wed. each month.

3d District (Westerly, Charlestown, Hopkinton and Richmond), *civil*, at Westerly each Fri.; Charlestown 4th Sat. each month; Hopkinton 2d and 4th Th. each month; Richmond 4th Wed. each month.

4th District (Kent Co.), *civil*, at Warwick each Tu.; East Greenwich each Th.; West Greenwich 3d Sat. each month; Coventry 2d and 4th Sat. each month.

5th District (Bristol Co.), *civil* at Bristol each Mon.; Warren each Th.

6th District (Providence and North Providence), *civil*, at Providence each Mon. and Th.

7th District (East Providence), *civil*, at East Providence each Fri.

8th District, (Johnston, Cranston, Scituate and Foster), *civil*, at Johnston each Mon.; Cranston each Wed.; Scituate, 3d Sat. each month; Foster 2d Sat. each month.

9th District (Burrillville, Smithfield and Glocester), *civil*, at Burrillville each Sat.; Smithfield each Th.; Glocester each Wed.

10th District (Pawtucket), *civil*, at Pawtucket each Tu. and Fri.

11th District (Central Falls, Lincoln and Cumberland), *civil*, at Central Falls Wed. and Sat. May adjourn any day to Lincoln or Cumberland.

12th District (Woonsocket and N'th Smithfield), *civil*, at Woonsocket each Wed. and Sat.

PROBATE COURTS.

In PROVIDENCE the Municipal Court is a Court of Probate. In other cities and towns which have not elected a Judge of Probate the city or town councils are Courts of Probate, having jurisdiction throughout such city or town with sittings as public interest may require. Where no other provision is made by law the city or town clerk is clerk of said court.

COURTS IN THE STATE OF CONNECTICUT.
(Corrected September, 1899.)

Supreme Court of Errors.

1st Judicial District. (Hartford, Windham, Tolland, Litchfield and Middlesex, Cos.) at Hartford, 1st Tu. Jan., Mar., May and Oct.

2d Dist. (New London Co.) at Norwich, last Tu. May and 3d Tu. Oct.

3d Dist. (New Haven, and Fairfield Cos.) at New Haven, 3d Tu. Jan., and 1st Tu. June; Bridgeport, 3d Tu. Apr. and 4th Tu. Oct.

Superior Court.

The Superior Court in each county is open daily, for certain purposes, except during July and August. *Additional sessions* may be fixed by the judges.

Fairfield Co., *civil*, at Danbury, 3d Tu. Jan. and Sept.; Bridgeport, 1st Tu. Jan. and Apr. and 2d Tu. Oct.; *crim.*, Bridgeport, 3d Tu. Feb. and 2d Tu. Sept.; Danbury, 2d Tu. May and 3d Tu. Oct.

Hartford Co., at Hartford, *civil*, 1st Tu. Jan. and Apr., 2d Tu. Oct.; *crim.*, 1st Tu. Mar., June and Dec., 2d Tu. Sept.

Litchfield Co., *civil and crim.*, at Litchfield, 1st Tu. Oct.; New Milford, 1st Tu. Apr.; Winchester, 1st Tu. Feb. and June.

Middlesex Co., *civil and crim.*, at Middletown, 4th Tu. Sept.; *crim.* Middletown, 1st Tu. Apr. and Dec.; *civil*, Middletown, 4th Tu. Jan. and 2d Tu. Apr. and Nov.

New Haven Co., *civil*, at New Haven, 1st Tu. Jan. and Apr. and 4th Tu. Sept.; Waterbury, *civil*, 1st Tu. May; *civil and crim.*, 3d Tu. Feb., June and Oct.; New Haven, *crim.*, 1st Tu. Jan., Apr., July and Oct.

New London Co., *civil*, at New London, 3d Tu. Sept.; Norwich, 4th Tu. May and 1st Tu. Nov.; *civil and crim.* New London, 2d Tu. Feb.; *crim.*, New London, 1st Tu. Sept.; Norwich, 1st Tu. Jan. and May.

Tolland Co., *civil and crim.*, at Tolland, 2d Tu. Apr. and 1st Tu. June, Sept. and Dec. Any session may be held at Rockville or at Stafford Springs, and may be adjourned to or from Tolland, Rockville or Stafford Springs, whenever deemed advisable.

Windham Co., *civil and crim.*, at Putnam, 1st Tu. Mar. and Sept.; Windham, 1st Tu. May and 3d Tu. Oct.

Courts of Common Pleas.

Fairfield Co., at Danbury, 1st Tu. Feb., Apr., June, Dec.; Bridgeport, 1st Tu. Jan., Mar., May, Sept., Oct., Nov.; and may adjourn from or to Danbury, Bridgeport, Norwalk or Stamford, as the business may require; *crim.*, at Bridgeport, 1st Tu. each mo. except July and Aug.; may adjourn to Danbury, Norwalk or Stamford.

Hartford Co., at Hartford, 1st Mo. Jan., Mar., May, Sept. and Nov.

Litchfield Co., at Litchfield, 1st. Tu. May and Nov.; Winchester, 1st Tu.Jan. and Sept.; Canaan, 1st Tu. Feb. and Oct.; New Milford, 1st Tu. Mar. and Dec.

COURTS IN CONNECTICUT (Continued).

New Haven Co., at New Haven, 1st Mo. Jan., Mar. May, and Nov. and 3d Mo. Sept.; *crim.*, 1st Mo. each month.

New London Co., at Norwich, 1st Tu. Feb. and Oct.; New London, 1st Tu. Apr. and Aug.; *crim.*, Norwich, 2d Tu. Feb. and Aug.; New London, 2d Tu. Apr. and Oct.

The District Court Of Waterbury includes Waterbury and towns adjoining. Terms, 1st Tu. Jan., till Fri. bef. 1st Mo. July; and 1st Tu. Sept., till Fri. bef. Dec. 25; *crim.*, 1st Tu. Mar., June, Sept. and Dec. Suits ret. 1st. Tu. ea. mo. except July and Aug.

PROBATE COURTS.

There is a Court of Probate in each probate district. No dates for holding probate courts are fixed by statute but they may be held as occasion requires at the discretion of the several judges of probate.

LEGISLATURES OF NEW ENGLAND STATES.

SESSIONS COMMENCE AS FOLLOWS:

Maine. First Wednesday of January 1901, and in each alternate year.
New Hampshire. First Wednesday of January 1901, and in each alternate year.
Vermont. Second Thursday of October 1900, and in each alternate year.
Massachusetts. First Wednesday of January of each year.
Rhode Island. Last Tuesday of May each year at Newport with adjournment to Providence.
Connecticut. Wednesday after the First Monday of January 1901, and in each alternate year.

THE PUBLIC DEBT, August 31, 1899.

Interest-bearing Debt	$1,046,048,850 00
Debt on which interest has ceased since maturity	1,215,150 26
Debt bearing no interest	389,395,427 16
Aggregate of interest and non-interest bearing Debt	1,436,659,427 42
Certificates and Treasury Notes offset by an equal amount of cash in the Treasury	601,443,203 00
Aggregate of Debt, including Certificates and Treasury Notes	2,038,102,630 42

Cash in the Treasury.

CLASSIFICATION.		DEMAND LIABILITIES.	
Gold — Coin	$189,986,759 58	Gold Certificates	$ 82,218,419 00
Bars	127,460,200 72	Silver Certificates	407,278,504 00
Silver — Dollars	416,364,995 00	Cert. of Dep., act June 8, 1872	19,430,000 00
Subsidiary Coin	4,130,191 96	Treasury Notes of 1890	92,516,280 00
Bars	84,564,627 17	Fund for red'ption of uncurrent Nat'l Bank Notes	9,399,173 64
Paper — United States Notes	36,550,595 00	Outstanding Checks and Drafts	5,946,662 95
Treasury Notes of 1890	865,648 00	Disbursing Officers' Balances	60,373,412 46
Gold Certificates	13,529,430 00	Agency Accounts, etc.	5,864,557 83
Silver Certificates	3,646,159 00		
Cert. of Dep., act June 8, 1872	260,000 00	**Gold Reserve**	**$100,000,000 00**
National Bank Notes	3,632,408 04	**Net Cash Balance**	**179,352,872 38**
Other— Bonds, interest and coupons paid, awaiting reimbursement	240,617 58		
Minor Coin and Fractional Currency	196,795 78		
Dep. Nat. Bank Depos. General Account	75,087,858 58		
Disbursing Officers' Balances	5,863,595 85		
Aggregate	$962,379,882 26	Aggregate	$962,379,882 26

CARRIAGE FARES IN BOSTON.

The hack rates for one adult, from one place to another within the city proper (with the exception of distances beyond certain limits, the rates for which are $1.00 and upwards, *see printed pamphlet of Regulations*) or from one place to another in East Boston, or from one place to another in South Boston, or from one place to another in Charlestown, or from one place to another in Roxbury, **50 cents.** Each additional adult, **50 cents.**

☞ Every person in charge of a hackney carriage is required to carry, so that it shall be accessible to passengers, a copy of the established rates.

Children under four years, with an adult, **no charge.**
Children between four and twelve years old, with an adult, **half-price.**
From twelve at night to six in the morning, the fare is **50 cents above the preceding rates** for each passenger.
No charge for one trunk; each additional trunk, **25 cents.**
The **cab rates** are in general one-half the hack rates.

INCREASE OF DEER IN NEW ENGLAND.

The increase of deer in the New England States in recent years has presented a point of great interest to persons fond of forest life. In Maine the increase has been remarkable, and within that State there is now an immensely greater number of deer than there was, say, thirty years ago.

The chief cause of this increase is undoubtedly the enforcement of proper laws regulating hunting. Having been for some years protected from indiscriminate slaughter, deer have multiplied to an extent beyond the most sanguine expectation. By the laws referred to it is sought to protect them from being hunted after the snow has become too deep and heavy for their escape, and to continue this protection through the breeding season and until the fawns are grown large enough to take care of themselves. The open seasons vary somewhat in the several New England States and adjacent British Provinces, which have open seasons, but generally, they may all be said to be included within the period from September first to January first. Even in the open season no one person may kill but a very limited number. These laws are not only on the statute books; they are enforced and meet public approval. The enforcement of the various game laws, supported by a hearty public sentiment, will early result in there being still greater numbers of deer and of the many other kinds of game, for the support of which in luxuriant abundance the beautiful country of New England is so well adapted.

(From U. S. Monthly Weather Review for May, 1897.)

WIND-BAROMETER TABLE.

BY E. B. GARRIOTT, Professor, Weather Bureau.

The following table presents, in form for ready reference, atmospheric signs which have been found to presage certain weather changes and conditions over the middle and upper Mississippi and lower Missouri valleys, the Great Lakes, the Ohio Valley, and the Middle Atlantic and New England States:

BAROMETER (REDUCED TO SEA LEVEL).	WIND DIRECTION.	CHARACTER OF WEATHER INDICATED.
30.00 to 30.20, and steady	westerly . .	Fair, with slight changes in temperature, for one to two days.
30.00 to 30.20, and rising rapidly	westerly . .	Fair, followed within two days by warmer and rain.
30.00 to 30.20, and falling rapidly	s. to e. . . .	Warmer, and rain within 24 hours.
30.20, or above, and falling rapidly . .	s. to e. . . .	Warmer and rain within 36 hours.
30.20, or above, and falling rapidly . .	w. to n.	Cold and clear, quickly followed by warmer and rain.
30.20, or above, and steady	variable	No early change.
30.00, or below, and falling slowly . . .	s. to e. . . .	Rain within 18 hours that will continue a day or two.
30.00, or below, and falling rapidly . .	se. to ne.	Rain, with high winds, followed within two days by clearing, colder.
30.00, or below, and rising	s. to w.	Clearing and colder within 12 hours.
29.80, or below, and falling rapidly . .	se to ne.	Severe storm of wind and rain imminent. In winter, snow and cold wave within 24 hours.
29.80, or below, and falling rapidly . .	e. to n.	Severe northeast gales and heavy rain or snow, followed, in winter, by cold wave.
29.80, or below, and rising rapidly . . .	going to w.	Clearing and colder.

The character of the precipitation, whether rain or snow, is governed by the temperature.

* * * * Local signs and observations, however, rarely indicate the duration and intensity of threatened atmospheric disturbances save in the immediate presence of a storm, and barometric readings are ofttimes misleading, unless considered in connection with the readings taken at points remote from the place of observation.

On Brougham's elevation to the highest judicial position in England, that of Lord Chancellor, a noted barrister said, "If Brougham only knew a little law, he would know a little of everything."

UNITED STATES INTERNAL REVENUE.
Legacy, Special and Stamp Taxes.

LEGACY TAXES.

When the whole amount of personal property is over $10,000, and not over $25,000, the tax is .75 to $5.00 on each $100.00, of the beneficial interest of each person according to degree of consanguinity, (husband and wife exempt).

Exceeding $25,000.00, the rates above should be multiplied as follows:

Over $25,000 and not over $100,000, by 1½.
" 100,000 " " " 500,000, " 2.
" 500,000 " " " 1,000,000, " 2½.
" 1,000,000 " 3.

SPECIAL TAXES.

Bankers, cap. and surplus $25,000
or less $50.00
each additional., $1000.00 . . . 2.00
Brewers, less than 500 bbls. . . 50.00
over 500 bbls. 100.00
Bowling and Billiards, each
alley or table 5.00
Brokers, ... 50.00
Commercial 20.00
Custom-house 10.00
Pawn 20.00
Cigars, per M. over 3 lbs. wt. . . 3.60
not " " " " . . 1.00
Manf's. according to ann. sales
. . . . 6.00 to 24.00
Cigarrettes, per M. over 3 lbs. wt. 3.60
not " " " 1.50
Circuses, ... 100.00
Exhibitions, for money 10.00
Filled Cheese, manufacturers . 400.00
Retail dealers 12.00
Wholesale dealers 250.00
Liquors, retail dealers 25.00
Wholesale dealers 100.00
Malt Liquors, per bbl. 2.00
Retail dealers 20.00
Wholesale dealers 50.00
Mixed Flour, Manf's. and packers 12.00
per bbl. 04
half " 02
fourth bbl. 01
eighth " 005
Oleomargarine, manufacturers 600.00
Retail dealers 48.00
Wholesale dealers 480.00
Rectifiers, less than 500 bbls. . 100.00
500 bbls. or more 200.00
Snuff, per lb. 12
Stills, manufacturers 50.00
each still and each worm . . 20.00
Theatres, etc., in cities over 25,-
000 pop. 100.00
Tobacco, per lb. 12
Dealers in leaf according to annual sales . . . . . $6.00 to 24.00
Dealers in manufactured, ann.
sales exceeding 50,000 lbs. . 12.00
Manufacturers according to annual sales. . . . . . 6.00 to 24.00

STAMP TAXES, SCHEDULE A.

Bank check, draft, certificate of deposit not drawing interest, or order for payment of a sum of money, at sight or on demand .02
Bill of Exchange (inland), draft certificate of deposit drawing interest, U.S. money order, or order for payment of a sum of money otherwise than at sight or on demand, or any promissory note, and for each renewal of same, not exceeding $100 02
Each additional $100, or fraction in excess thereof 02
(foreign), or letter of credit (including orders by telegraph, or otherwise), drawn in, but payable out of the U.S., drawn singly or otherwise than in sets of three or more, not exceeding $100 . . .04
Each additional $100 or fraction in excess thereof , ...04
Drawn in sets of two or more, for every bill of each set not exceeding $100 or its equivalent in foreign currency, value fixed by the U.S. standard 02
Each additional $100 or frac. .02
Bills of Lading, or receipt for goods, etc., to be exported except Brit. N.A. 10
Manifests, etc., issued by express companies or public carriers, and each duplicate thereof .01
Bonds, debentures or certificates of indebtedness each $100 or fraction 05
Bond, indemnifying, etc., except those required in legal proceedings, not otherwise provided for .50
Certificate, of damage or otherwise, and all other certificates or documents issued by port warden or marine surveyor . . .25
Of stock (original issue), each $100 or fraction 05
Of profits or memorandum showing interest in property or accumulations of any association, etc., and all transfers thereof, each $100 or fraction . .02
Required by law; not otherwise specified 10
Charter party, contract or agreement for the charter of any vessel or the renewal thereof, not exceeding 300 tonnage . . 3.00
More than 300 and not exceeding 600 tonnage 5.00
More than 600 tonnage . . . 10.00
Contract, brokers, etc., note or memorandum of sale, not otherwise provided for 10
Conveyance, deed, instrument or writing conveying lands, tenements or other realty, value over $100 not over $500 50
Each additional $500 or fraction 50
Dispatch, telegraphic, each message 01
Entry, of merchandise in custom house, not over $100 in value . .25
Exceeding $100 not exceeding $500 50
Exceeding $500 . . . . . . 1.00
For withdrawal of merchandise from customs bonded warehouse 50
Insurance, life, on every policy, except fraternal beneficiary,

Insurance continued.

etc., each $100 or fraction of amount insured 08

Industrial or weekly payment plan, 40 per centum of amount of first weekly premium . . .

Marine, inland and fire (except co-operative or mutual), each policy or renewal, on each $1 or fraction of prem. charged   .00½

Casualty, fidelity and guarantee, each $1 or fraction of prem. charged 00½

Lease, agreement or contract for hire or rent of land or tenement, not exceeding one year. 25

Exceeding one year and not three years 50

Exceeding three years . · ·   1.00

Manifest, for custom house entry or clearance of cargo of any vessel for a foreign port except ports in Brit. N.A., registered tonnage not exceeding 300 tons   1.00

Exceeding 300 and not exceeding 600 tons 3.00

Exceeding 600 tons. 5.00

Mortgage or pledge, and assignment or transfer, of property, real or personal, or conveyance of same, as security, exceeding $1000 and not more than $1500 .   .25

Each $500 or fraction in excess of $1500 25

Passage Tickets, by vessel to a foreign port, except Brit. N.A., according to cost . . . . . . $1 to 5

Power of attorney, or proxy for voting for officers of any incorporated company or association, except religious, etc., ...10

To sell and convey, or rent, or lease, or collect rent of, real estate, or to sell or transfer stocks, bonds, etc. 25

Protest, of every note, bill of exchange, check, draft or marine protest 25

Sales, agreements to sell, memoranda of sales, deliveries or transfers of shares or certificates of stock, each $100 of face value or fraction thereof 02

Of any products or merchandise at any exchange or board of trade, etc., each $100 in value, and each additional $100 or fractional part. 01

Telephone messages, each costing 15 cents or more 01

Warehouse receipt for property in storage, except agricultural products deposited by actual grower 25

Whenever any bond or note is secured by mortgage, or deed of trust, but one stamp is required on such papers; provided that stamp tax placed thereon shall be the highest rate required for said instruments or either of them.

Upon each and every assignment or transfer of a mortgage, lease, or policy of insurance, or the renewal or continuance of any agreement, contract, or charter, by letter or otherwise, a stamp duty shall be required and paid, at the same rate as that imposed on the original instrument.

SCHEDULE B.

Chewing Gum, and substitutes; each package retail value not over $1.00 04

Each add'l $1.00 or fraction .   .04

Medicinal Proprietary Articles, Perfumery and Cosmetics, each package retail value 5 cents 00⅛

5 to 10 cents . . , ...00¼

10 to 15 cents 00⅜

15 to 25 " 00½

Each add'l 25 or fraction .   .00⅝

Seats and Berths, in Parlor and sleeping cars. 01

Wines, bottled, each pint or less   .01

Over one pint 02

THE TRANSCONTINENTAL ARC.

There has lately been completed by the Coast and Geodetic Survey, Washington, D.C., the computation of the transcontinental arc, the eastern terminal point of which is at Cape May, New Jersey, close to the Atlantic coast, and the western at Point Arena, California, close to the Pacific coast. These stations are about 2,625 miles apart as measured on the parallel of 39° north latitude, but the distance following the line of the survey is necessarily much greater. The probable error in the whole distance resulting from the computation is about the 1-150,000 part of the length, which is between 1-4 and 1-2 inch per mile. The field work was commenced in 1871 and completed in 1898. The line traverses fifteen states, and up to this time, it is the longest measure on record.

The results of this great work will be of both practical and scientific value. It will give numerous accurate geographical positions along an extended line crossing fifteen states, and furnish a basis for state and local surveys; it will firmly connect the surveys of the eastern and western parts of the United States, furnish means to fit and adjust them with each other, thus establishing uniform geodetic data; and it will give a most valuable contribution of data for the determination of the earth's figure and size, the United States being a member of the International Geodetic Association, which has this particular object in view.

44

POETRY, ANECDOTES, HUMOR, Etc.

GOD-SPEED TO THE SNOW.

MARCH is slain; the keen winds fly;
Nothing more is thine to do,
April kisses thee good-bye;
Thou must haste and follow too;
Silent friend that guarded well
Withered things to make us glad,
Shyest friend that could not tell
Half the kindly thought he had.
Haste thee, speed thee, O kind snow,
Down the dripping valleys go,
From the fields and gleaming meadows,
Where the slaying hours behold thee,
From the forests whose dim shadows,
Brown and leafless, cannot fold thee,
Through the cedar lands aflame
With gold light that cleaves and quivers,
Songs that winter may not tame,
Drone of pines and laugh of rivers.
May thy passing joyous be
To thy father, the great sea,
For the sun is getting stronger;
Earth hath need of thee no longer;
Go, kind snow, God-speed to thee!
ARCHIBALD LAMPMAN.

THE NEW MEMORIAL DAY.

Oh, the roses we plucked for the blue,
And the lilies we twined for the gray,
We have bound in a wreath,
And in silence beneath
Slumber our heroes to-day.

Over the new-turned sod
The sons of our fathers stand,
And the fierce old fight
Slips out of sight
In the clasp of a brother's hand.

For the old blood left a stain
That the new has washed away,
And the sons of those
That have faced as foes
Are marching together to-day.

Oh, the blood that our fathers gave!
Oh, the tide of our mothers' tears!
And the flow of red
And the tears they shed
Embittered a sea of years.

But the roses we plucked for the blue,
And the lilies we twined for the gray,
We have bound in a wreath,
And in glory beneath
Slumber our heroes to-day
ALBERT BIGELOW PAINE.

AN INSULT.

"YOU see," said the man from southern California, "you eastern men don't give us a fair show, to begin with. You start out on the idea that we are all liars about our big trees and vegetables, and you not only encourage a man to exaggerate, but go back on him when he falls into the trap."

"Well, now, but what I'm after is facts," replied the other. "I've heard about your big squashes, and I want to know how large a one you ever saw?"

"You want the cold truth."

"I do. If you have seen one as big as a barn, don't hesitate to say so."

"But I'm afraid you'll charge me with exaggeration."

"No, I wont. I know you have wonderful soil, and a still more wonderful climate, and I've seen some of your big fruits and vegetables with my own eyes. You must have seen a champion squash in your day."

"Well, to be honest, I have, but when I started from home last week I determined to keep my mouth shut about our wonderful products. I can give you the name of a man in Los Angeles who will—"

"I don't want to open no correspondence," interrupted the other. "You saw the big squash yourself, and I've said I'd take your word for it. Was it as big as a four-room cottage?"

"I—I—hardly think so."

"Was it as big as a haystack?"

"I wouldn't want to say it was."

"Don't be afraid to give dimensions. Was it as big as four hogsheads put together?"

"I'm afraid not."

"As large as two?"

"No, I don't think it was."

"But it must have been as large as a hogshead!" indignantly exclaimed the easterner.

"It was a champion squash, and it was a whopper," replied the Californian, "but it wasn't as large as that. You've seen a beer keg, of course—one holding an eighth of a barrel?"

"Certainly I have, but you don't mean to tell me that your whopping old champion squash—"

"Was exactly the size of one of those kegs. I measured it myself. It was taken to the state fair, and the papers made a great fuss over it, and it—"

"You will excuse me, sir!" interrupted the easterner as he rose up with flushed face, "but we will not continue the conversation any further! When my own wife spent a whole winter in a California squash divided into three stories and fourteen large and airy rooms your dimensions and comparisons are an insult to my intelligence—an insult to my intelligence, sir!"

I HAVE heard a story, says a western paper, of a sad occurrence to a Boston lady of great respectability. This lady was recently travelling to the Pacific coast over the Northern Pacific Railroad. Now North Dakota is a rigid prohibition State, and the dining cars have this notice posted up in them, "No intoxicating liquors will be served while the train is passing through the State of North Dakota." The train had been rolling along through that interminable State a long time, when the Boston lady who is interested in temperance came into the dining car for her dinner. Casting her eye out of the car window upon a somewhat changed landscape, she said to the waiter, with purely geographical interest:

"Are we still in North Dakota?"

"No, ma'am," said he alertly and with a hospitable grin; "what'll you take to drink, ma'am?"

METHINKS the world is sweeter than of
 yore,   [ing fair;
 More fresh and fine, and more exceed-
There is a presence never felt before,
 The soul of inspiration everywhere;
Incarnate youth in every idle limb,
 My vernal days, my prime, return
  anew;
My tranced spirit breathes a silent
  hymn,
 My heart is full of dew!
      R. H. STODDARD.

"I SUPPOSE it was a perfectly natural
feeling I had when I returned from
Europe," said the Boston drummer,
"and that feeling, of course, was to let
everybody know I had made the trip.
No doubt I made a good many folks tired,
but I got the knock-out when I least expected it. I was down Cape Cod way to
visit a brother, and one day entered a
village store where half a dozen farmers
were sitting around. I managed to get
the conversation around to "Yurup,"
and as they were all good listeners I
had the floor to myself for half an hour.
I told them of London, Paris, Rome,
Venice and all that, and not one of them
asked a single question. I hadn't got
tired out yet, but had paused to get a
better hold, when an old gray-head with
the soberest face you ever saw looked
up and queried :

"'So stranger, ye've crossed the
ocean?'

"'Yes sir.'

"'And seen all them places in Yurup?'

"'Yes.'

"'And got back as slick as grease?'

"'As you see.'

"'Wall, that's powerful smart of ye,'
he continued, 'but I'd like to ask ye a
question or two. How high is a six-
rail fence?'"

"I had to reply that I didn't know.

"How much does a bushel of wheat
weigh?'

"'I wasn't sure within five pounds."

"When does a baby get its first
tooth?

"I was stumped on that and said so."

"'Then I'll ask ye some easy ones,'
he said. 'How many 'taters does a
farmer plant in a hill?'

"'I can't say.'

"'What's the object in heving the
front wheels of a wagon the smallest?'

"'I give it up.'

"'How long does it take chickens to
hatch?'

"'I never knew.'

"'Which end does a horse get up on
first.'

"'I—I never watched.'

"The old man and the crowd turned
from me in contempt," said the drummer, "and feeling at least a foot shorter
than when I went in I edged for the
door. My questioner had something in
reserve, however. As I reached the
door he called, —

"'Wall, stranger, mebbe you wasn't
so much to blame fur goin to Yurup,
bein' ye had the time and money, but
fur the next year or two I'll be won-
derin' why on airth you didn't stay over
there the rest o' yer days?'"

ONE OF KIPLING'S ANCESTORS.

MR. KIPLING, says the *New York
Times*, comes of Methodist ancestry "on
both sides of the house," as they say
Down East, and perhaps elsewhere.
His paternal grandfather was the Rev.
Joseph Kipling, a member of a well-to-
do farming family in Cumberland. The
other grandfather was the Rev. George
B. Macdonald, also a Wesleyan clergy-
man, but of an altogether different
type. It is related of this Macdonald
that in the days when he was courting
the lady whom he afterward married,
the father-in-law-to-be— an aged Methodist, with extremely strict notions in
regard to the proprieties— was injudi-
cious enough on one occasion to enter
the parlor without giving any warning
of his approach.

The consequence was that he found
the sweethearts occupying a single
chair. Deeply shocked by this spectacle,
the old man solemnly said; "Mr. Macdonald, when I was courting Mrs. Brown
she sat on one side of the room and I
on the other side." Macdonald's reply
was; "That's what I should have done
if I had been courting Mrs. Brown."

A SPARROW IN WINTER.

BLITHELY on the gray rose tree
Hear the sparrow cheep in glee!
Though no roses bloom and blow
On the branch that's rimmed with snow,
He remembers how the roses
 Gaily glimmered,
 Shyly shimmered,
Where the snowflake now reposes;
And he fancies he can see
Butterfly and bumblebee,
 Rapture brimming,
 Idly skimming
Round the roses on the tree,
If he can the roses spy
With his fancy's searching eye,
Then the roses for him blow,
Though the way is deep with snow —
Though the north wind whines and
  whistles,
 And the dust of silver whirls
O'er the crisp and shriveled thistles,
 Where the cold the leaflet curls.
Only roses bloom for him
On the frail and fragile limb,
And the nest sways to and fro
In the starlit afterglow —
When his lively fancy sees
Rose flakes tremble in the breeze.
All his dream's a prescience gay
Of the coming of the May,
When the blossoms pink and white,
E'er a vision of delight,
 Zephyr shaken,
 Burst to waken
Song from dewy dawn till night—
Then he'll sing with joyful zest
To his happy new-found mate,
While they build the swinging nest
 In the rose tree at the gate.
What cares he how winter moans,
In its dismalest of tones,
When he sees the roses twinkle,
 As the wind steals from the west,
All the dewy flakes to sprinkle
 Round and round the love-built nest?
    Woman's Home Companion

AN EASY-GOIN' FELLER.

It somehow seems to me a friend that's
  worth my cultivatin'
Should have a host o' stories that he's
  allers glad to tell,
An' make your sides ache laughin' in the
  office while you're waitin'
An' ask you sorter careless if the folks
  at home are well;
A feller who'll advise you how to cure
  the croup or ague,
Or maybe tell you what to do with
  horses that'll balk,
A chap who'll crack a joke on you an'
  allers like to plague you,
An easy-goin' feller who will sit aroun'
  an' talk.

I never had no patience with a man
  that's cold an' steelly,
Who comes an' goes to business on a
  dog trot, all alone;
He may be tender-hearted, but you're
  bound to allers feel he
Don't take a mite o' interest in no
  troubles but his own.
I like to have a friend who asks how
  well along I'm gettin',
Who allers got a word to sorter cheer
  you when you're frettin',
An easy-goin' feller who will sit aroun'
  an' talk.

Jes such a friend one likes to have if
  son or daughter marry,
He's allers sayin' somethin' for to
  cheer 'em on their way;
It's such a friend you like to see when
  called upon to bury
The one you swore to love, protect, for-
  ever an' a day.
He isn't very offish, you know allers
  where to find him,
He's jes as plain an' common as a
  thumb-worn piece o' chalk;
You jes can't help but slap his back, a
  comin' up behind him—
An easy-goin' feller who will sit aroun'
  an' talk.
        Detroit Free Press.

The yearly miracle of Spring,
  Of budding tree and blooming flower,
Which Nature's feathered laureates sing
  In my cold ear, from hour to hour,
Spreads all its wonders round my feet;
  And every wakeful sense is fed
On thoughts that, o'er and o'er, repeat
  "The resurrection of the dead!"
        George H. Boker.

The shadow upon her husband's brow
was become habitual now, and it deep-
ened day by day.
  "Am I as dear to you as I used to
be?" she suddenly asked him once, for
her misgivings left her no peace of
mind.
  The man shivered, but he would fain
be candid with her.
  "Everything is dearer in the suburbs
than anywhere else!" he exclaimed,
taking her hand in his, and looking
steadfastly down into her great, gray
eyes.   *Puck.*

A popular drummer of the West at-
tended a large party one evening, and
after supper was over was promenad-
ing with one of the guests, a young
lady from the East, to whom he had
just been introduced.
  In the course of the conversation the
subject of business callings came up,
and she said:
  "By the way, Mr.——may I ask what
your occupation is?"
  "Certainly," he answered. "I am a
commercial traveler."
  "How very interesting! Do you know,
Mr.——, that in the part of the country
where I reside commercial travelers are
not received in good society?"
  Quick as a flash he rejoined:
  "They are not here, either, madam."
        Youth's Companion.

Flossy. I don't care, I think Jack
Townley is real mean!
  Annette. Why, Flossy?
  Flossy. He wrote to me from Florida,
saying he had shot an alligator seven
feet long, and said when he had shot
another he would have a pair of slippers
made for me.   *Harlem Life.*

The morning drum-call on my eager ear
Thrills unforgotten yet; the morning
  dew
Lies yet undried along my field of
  noon.
But now I pause at whiles in what I do,
And count the bell, and tremble lest I
  hear
(My work untrimmed) the sunset gun
  too soon.   R. L. Stevenson.

VERNAL PROPHECIES.

To-day the wind has a milder range,
And seems to hint of a secret change;
For the gossipy breezes bring to me
The delicate odor of buds to be
  In the gardens and groves of spring.

Those forces of nature we cannot see—
The procreant power in plant and tree,
Shall bring at last to the waiting thorn
The wealth of the roses yet unborn
  In the gardens and groves of spring.

The early grass in a sheltered nook
Unsheathes its blades near the forest
  brook;
In the first faint green of the elm I see
A gracious token of leaves to be
  In the gardens and groves of spring.

The peach trees brighten the river's
  brink,
With their dainty blossoms of white and
  pink,
And over the orchard there comes to me
The subtle fragrance of fruit to be
  In the gardens and groves of spring.

The rigor of winter has passed away,
While the earth seems yearning to meet
  her May,
And the voice of a bird in melodious glee
Foretells the sweetness of songs to be
  In the gardens and groves of spring.
        William Hamilton Hayne.

I HAVE but few companions on the
shore;
They scorn the strand who sail upon
the sea;
Yet oft I think the ocean they've sailed
o'er
Is deeper known upon the strand to
me.

The middle sea contains no crimson
dulse,
Its deeper waves cast up no pearls to
view;
Along the shore my hand is on its pulse,
And I converse with many a ship-
wrecked crew.   *Thoreau.*

ANSWERS TO PUZZLES, Etc., IN LAST YEAR'S ALMANAC.

ANSWERS TO CHARADES.

1. Chestnut. 2. Mendicant. 3. Moscow.

ANSWERS TO CONUNDRUMS.

1. Smiles, because there is a mile between the first and last letters.
2. Because they are continually crossing the line, and running from pole to
pole.
3. When he took a hack at the cherry
tree.
4. Herein.

ANSWERS TO PUZZLES.

1. Ten.
2. 9, 8, 7, 6, 5, 4, 3, 2, 1 = 45.
   1, 2, 3, 4, 5, 6, 7, 8, 9 = 45.
   8, 6, 4, 1, 9, 7, 5, 3, 2 = 45.
3. Twenty.

ANSWERS TO ANAGRAMS.

1. Presbyterians.
2. Felicity.
3. Spare him not.
4. Maidenly.

CHARADES.

1. My first is one of Neptune's arms;
   My second shows emotion;
Within my third come captive swarms
Of fishes from the ocean.

My whole goes foremost, keen and cold,
When angry nations quarrel;
And like the old Gambrinus bold,
It sits upon a barrel.
   Boston Charades.
      By [HERBERT INGALLS.]

2. My first and second Virgil sang;
   My third in old-time garden sprang;
   My fourth, if added to your hall,
   Might rouse the echoes with its call;
   My whole, a curious delver found
   Encased in armor 'neath the ground.
   A Second Century of Charades.
      [By WILLIAM BELLAMY.]

3. Words eloquent and gestures fine
   Compose my first, please note!
An article my second is,
My third you all will vote

To be the watchword of success;
And if life's cares and bitterness
Press all too hard, you'll surely find
My whole will solace your wrought
   mind.   *Boston Herald.*

4. My first is company,
   My second shuns company,
   My third assembles company,
   My whole amuses company. —*Do.*

RIDDLES.

1. My first is in rap, but not in knock;
   My second is in time, but not in clock;
   My third is in rain, but not in snow;
   My fourth is in wind, but not in blow;
   My fifth is in clown, but not in fool;
   My sixth is in chisel, and also in tool;
   My seventh is in Athens, and also in
      Rome;
   My eighth is in spray, but not in foam;
   My whole was the first to pay the sol-
diers and civil officers of ancient
Athens.

2. We are little airy creatures,
   All of different voice and features;
   One of us in glass is set,
   And a second found in jet;
   One of us is cased in tin,
   And the fourth a box within;
   If the fifth you would pursue,
   It can never fly from you.

3. What God never sees; what a King
seldom sees; what we see every day.

PUZZLES.

1. The number 45 has some curious
properties. Among others, it may be
divided into four parts, in such manner
that if you add two to the first, subtract two from the second, multiply the
third by two, and divide the fourth by
two, the result will in each case be
equal. What are they?
2. Required to find a number which
multiplied by 3, 6, 9, 12, 15, 18, 21, 24, or
27, shall in each case give no product the
same digit, three times repeated.
3. Required of the numbers 1, 2, 3, 4,
5, 6, 7, 8, 9, 0, to combine two fractions,
whose sum shall be equal to unity, each
number to be used once, and once only.
4. Required to divide the number 237
into three parts in such manner that
three times the first shall be equal to
five times the second and eight times
the third.
5. How many hard boiled eggs can a
man eat on an empty stomach?

CONUNDRUMS.

1. Why was the giant Goliath very
much astonished when David hit him
with a stone?
2. Why is Neptune like a searcher
after the philosopher's stone?
3. How did Henry VIII. differ as a
suitor from other men?
4. Why has the shoemaker wonderful
powers of endurance?
5. Which is the gayest letter of the
alphabet?
6. Which is heavier a half, or a full
moon?

LOOKING AFTER HIRED HELP ON THE FARM.

At such times as it becomes necessary to employ an overseer to look after a half dozen or more workmen, it is often difficult to get a man who is fully equal to the requirements of the position. One reason why this is so is because a very large number of those who would make good overseers are already in business on their own farms, or are young men who have yet many points to learn relating to the best way of treating men, to keep them satisfied with fair pay for the work given them to do, and contented under the admonitions which it is sometimes necessary to give them.

No man is fully qualified to direct others who has not full control over himself, even under the most trying circumstances. Whatever corrections he has to make, should always be made kindly, and with intelligence. Unkind words never improve the disposition of workmen, and very rarely improve their actions. An overseer should be fully competent to do any part of the work he directs others to do. If he is not, his ignorance is soon discovered and his power over his workmen greatly weakened. He should be able to judge correctly what is a fair day's work, and should be very careful not to accuse a workman of not doing a day's work when he has done all that he ought to do. An overseer should never assume airs of superiority and look down upon his workmen; but he should recognize and treat them as men, and by pleasant words adapted to their intelligence, lead them to thoughts which will tend, not only to make them more contented with their positions, but to cause them to do their work with more ease, and in a better manner. Do not treat farm laborers as though they were slaves, but treat them as free men who are supposed to be able to do well the work that is given them without having an overseer standing over them continually urging them to work faster. This may be necessary in some lines of work where cheap ignorant laborers are employed in large numbers, but it does not apply to the farm laborers of New England.

To clean plaster of Paris, mix a small cupful of whitening with hot water until of the consistency of thick cream, then with a small brush, paint the cast all over evenly with the mixture. A little isinglass may be mixed with the water to make the wash stay on. Melt this in a little hot water before it be added to the mixture.

As illustrating how dependent the native of Hindustan is upon instruction to the last degree of detail as to his duties under modern ways and methods, they tell of one of them occupying a subordinate position at one of the railway stations out in the country in India, who sent to railroad head-quarters the following telegram: "Tiger eating station master on front platform. Wire instructions."

Lemon juice, sweetened with loaf or crushed sugar, will relieve a cough.

If man could have half his wishes he would double his troubles. — BENJAMIN FRANKLIN.

Referring to the positive opinions on all subjects habitually expressed by Macaulay, the historian, Lord Melbourne is said to have remarked, "I wish I was as cocksure of anything as Tom Macaulay is of everything."

Some men were sitting in a grocery in the far West. One of them said, "I was out in camp last week and about nine o'clock one morning struck the trail of a big grizzly about half a mile from the camp. I followed that trail without let-up until about half past five in the afternoon, and then I quit."

"What made you give up after putting in so much hard work?" asked one of the company.

"Well, to tell the truth," said the first speaker, "that trail was getting entirely too fresh."

SPRAYING TREES TO KILL INSECTS AND TO DESTROY FUNGI.

THE people of the United States are progressive, and are not satisfied with only such productions as grow naturally in our country, but thoroughly search all foreign countries for such trees, shrubs and vines, as are supposed to be of any value, and import them hither. In doing this, a multitude of destructive insects are imported with them. So wonderfully prolific are some of these insects, that to save our crop of fruit, we are driven to the necessity of discovering new poisonous compounds, and new methods of application.

The race between man and the insects is a very even one, and man keeps but a short distance in advance; yet thus far he has been able to devise some way to destroy, or at least greatly to reduce the number of each new insect, soon after he makes his appearance.

When the European currant worm appeared, it was but a short time before white hellebore was discovered to be an effectual remedy when dusted on the bushes at just the right time, and in the right manner; but it was some years before unobserving persons discovered that the first crop of worms come about the tenth of May, and that they are always on a few leaves in the centre of the bush, near the ground, where they can be easily killed by dusting on a small quantity of hellebore.

When the Colorado potato beetle came, it was soon found to be proof against hellebore, but it did not take long to discover that Paris green would kill him; but it was also found that if too much Paris green be applied, it would kill the leaves of potatoes, and also the leaves of trees. So when applied to the leaves of trees and shrubs to kill various insects, it was found very difficult to prepare the Paris green and water in just the right proportions to kill the insects without injuring the leaves of the trees. A small teaspoonful of Paris green is sufficient for two gallons of water. Never apply cold water to any plant, but have the water nearly as warm as the air is at the time of application.

Arsenate of lead promises to be a better material than Paris green for the destruction of insects; it can be used very strong without any injury to vegetation, and it will remain on the leaves a much longer time than Paris green. For the destruction of the Gypsy moth, it is the best poison yet discovered.

During the past ten years, in some sections of the country, fruit trees have been very seriously injured by fungi which appear on the leaves of the trees, and also on the fruit, in our orchards. The remedy for this is not easy, but spraying with Bordeaux mixture is a great help to the trees, if commenced early and continued every week or two during the summer. Whether by following this for several seasons in succession, the fungi can be stamped out, remains yet to be proved. Unless growers find some effectual remedy for this enemy to the fruit tree and the fruit, there are some sections of the country where it will be difficult to grow fruit of the first quality.

As new discoveries are being made every year, it is fair to presume that man will soon be able to conquer this pest of the orchard.

The San Jose Scale is comparatively a new pest that promises to be very difficult to eradicate from the orchard, without digging up the trees, and burning both root and branch.

Bordeaux Mixture: How to make it: Dissolve six pounds of sulphate of copper in sixteen gallons of water. Slack four pounds of quicklime with six gallons of water When the slacked lime is cooled, mix it thoroughly with the copper mixture, then strain through a fine sieve or coarse cloth, and before using add to it fifty-six gallons of water. Stir frequently while using it, to prevent the lime from settling. Use freely to spray trees that show a fungus growth on them; but do not spray while the trees are in blossom, or when the young fruit is forming.

Bordeaux mixture can be purchased ready made at most of the agricultural stores, and if one is to use only small quantities, it is cheaper to buy it ready mixed; but when large orchards are to be sprayed, the farmer will find it for his interest to make it.

WINDMILLS FOR THE ELEVATION OF WATER.

IN towns where water is not distributed by public water works, and where good water from neighboring hills cannot be drawn by gravity through pipes to the farm in sufficient quantities to supply the farmers' wants, a good windmill where there is plenty of water that can be pumped into an elevated reservoir, will soon pay its cost in the saving of time necessary to pump and carry the water required even for domestic purposes, to say nothing of the amount the farmer may need for his flower and vegetable gardens. As there is not always wind enough to carry the pump, a wooden tank should be provided that will hold from 500 to 2000 gallons of water, according to size of windmill, and to the amount of water required. A two days' supply of water in most localities is sufficient; there is rarely more than twenty-four hours in succession when there is not wind enough to carry a ten foot wind mill, with a pump attached, that will pump the water thirty feet high. The tank should be elevated at least four feet higher than the highest point where the water is to be used. While the pipes and pump should be well protected from the frost, the tank will only require a building of matched boards about it large enough to leave six inches space between it and the tank, to keep the water from freezing, in the coldest weather, unless for some reason no water is pumped in for a period of more than twenty-four hours.

If kept properly oiled, the expense of running a windmill is very small indeed. A ten foot mill, if it be a good one, will pump, on an average, 5000 gallons per day, lifting the water thirty feet high. A good mill with pump, pipe and tank will cost from $150 to $250 according to size and length of pipe. The best mills are the cheapest in the end.

SOWING GRASS SEED IN AUGUST.

THERE are many reasons why it is best to sow grass seed in August. Sown at this season, the weeds will not choke out the young grass as they will in the Spring months. If the land be somewhat wet, it can be ploughed better in August than at any other season of the year. Moreover in August many farmers have more leisure than in the Spring. If the land be grass land, and it is ploughed to reseed it, by doing so in August the first crop will have been harvested, and the seed can be sown sufficiently early to give the young grass time to get so well established before winter, that it will be in a condition to produce a good crop next July. Thus the land may be reseeded with the loss of but one crop, and that a second crop; but if ploughed in the Spring, the first crop would be lost, and not a large second crop obtained.

Occasionally we have a dry season which interferes with August seeding. On high land it is very difficult to seed down to grass in the Spring unless it be done as soon as the frost is out of the ground. At this time a good catch can sometimes be obtained, and the young grass get the advantage of the weeds; but there will be some weeds that will get the advantage of the grass in portions of the field. As a rule it pays the farmer to reseed his land once every six or eight years.

PREPARING PRODUCE FOR MARKET.

THE farmer who depends on the Commission Merchant to sell the produce of his farm, should ever keep in mind the fact that no work on the farm will pay better than that expended in properly assorting and packing in an attractive form, the produce that is to be thus sold. He should not only be particular to have each grade as uniform as possible, but the best grade should be put in new, attractive packages, and he should put his name and the name of the farm on each package. The appearance of a package, and the manner in which the produce is packed, often make a difference in the price which it will command that will amount to a fair profit. To secure ready sales at fair prices a reputation for careful and honest packing must be acquired. This can best be done by marking each package with the producer's name.

GROWING CHESTNUTS AND SHELLBARKS FOR THE MARKET.

IN some portions of New England, a young man with a few hundred dollars to invest, can by investing it in an orchard of nut trees, be reasonably sure in from thirty to fifty years, of getting a larger per cent. interest than what is considered at the present time a high rate.

The chestnut is very easily grown from the seed; but in many portions of New England it would be easy to find chestnut forests that could be purchased very cheap. By cutting out all other trees, and thinning out the chestnut trees where they are found too thick, in a few years the trees would begin to bear fruit in sufficient quantities to show quite a good profit to the owner. And as the trees increase in size, if the small ones be cut out to give the large ones room, the product would increase.

The chestnut grows best on strong land; but it will make a fair growth and produce considerable fruit on loamy land. It seems to prefer rich valleys.

To grow shellbarks it is more difficult to get trees of good quality than of any fruit we grow, but when this difficulty is overcome, the crop becomes not only a very sure one, but a very profitable one. To get good trees, it is best to plant the seed, and when the trees are about half an inch in diameter within six inches of the ground, bud them with the best variety of shellbarks that can be found. In varieties there is a great choice; while some are large with thin shells and finely flavored meat, others are small, with thick shells and poorly flavored meat. The thin shelled nut is the best. An orchard of trees, where all produced good fruit, would be very profitable after it had grown twenty-five or thirty years.

The walnut tree grows best on high land with a strong soil and somewhat rocky. Land too full of large boulders to admit of being ploughed, would seem to be the most desirable place in which to grow walnut trees.

KILLING WEEDS.

No farmer should grow two crops on any particular portion of his farm at the same time, and have one of them weeds. There are few, if any conditions under which it is economy to let the weeds grow as high as the crop, even when the crop is less than one inch high. There are at the present time so many implements that are better for killing weeds than the old hand hoe, that the farmer is not wise who lets the weeds grow until they overshadow his crops. It is economy to run the weeder over garden crops when small, at least twice a week; not only to kill the weeds as soon as they appear above ground, but also to stir the surface of the soil to prevent its forming a hard crust, and to secure a rapid growth.

TREES AND SHRUBS AROUND THE DWELLING HOUSE.

TREES and shrubs, when properly arranged around the dwelling house are always pleasing objects to passers by; and the dwellers in a house thus beautified, will return to it with a higher regard, and greater love for it, than they would to a home not made attractive by objects of nature arranged by persons of intelligence and good taste.

In arranging the trees and shrubs, care should be taken to secure the greatest benefit to the inmates of the home. While the winter sun should not be shut out by shade trees, the mid-day summer sun may be, at least partially, shut out to advantage. Never therefore set evergreen trees on the south side of the house, and deciduous trees on the north side. Nor should evergreen shrubs be set very near the south side of the house. All trees that grow very large should be set from thirty to fifty feet from the house; an American Elm should be at least fifty feet from any building.

If the lawn be large, as it should be in the country towns, a border of evergreen trees should be set on the north side of the dwelling, for both beauty and shelter. The Hemlock, White Pine and Red Cedar, are good varieties for this purpose. For deciduous trees, the Purple Beech, Sugar Maple and White Ash make good varieties. As the number of varieties of trees desirable to plant depends very much on location and extent of grounds, those about to ornament their grounds with trees and shrubs, should make themselves familiar enough with the subject to be able to make such selections as are best adapted to the locality and size of the premises. Of flowering shrubs there are so many good varieties that selections should be made during the season when each variety is in blossom, making a list of the names of those that are preferred, and keeping it to be referred to when the season for transplanting arrives.

To prepare the soil for trees and shrubs, remove the earth where the tree or shrub is to set to a depth of eighteen inches in a circular space twice the diameter of the spread of the roots, and not less than four feet in diameter, whatever may be the spread of the roots; fill the hole with rich loam, mixed with equal parts of fine decomposed muck that has been exposed to the air long enough to remove all of the acid which was in it when dug. Never mix fresh manure with the muck or loam unless it be done at least two months before the trees are to be planted. Whatever manure is applied at the time of setting the trees, should be placed very near the surface after the roots are covered, or on the surface, and immediately covered with a heavy mulch of leaves or small evergreen boughs. If the soil be dry, the trees should be watered once a week during the summer and early autumn months, the first and second years after they are planted. As a rule, trees more than six feet high need to be watered the second year quite as much as the first.

Trees that have no leaves to shade the trunk from three to six feet from the ground, should have their trunks covered with one thickness of coarse bagging to prevent the sun from burning them.

THE SEASON FOR CUTTING THE WHITE PINE.
(Pinus Strobus.)

MANY years of close observation with numerous, carefully tried experiments, show that the white pine should be cut in August, September or October to secure the best quality of lumber. If cut during either of these months the logs may lay where cut all the following season without being eaten by worms. But if cut in either February, March or April, unless the logs be put in water soon after being cut, and kept there until sawed, the worms will eat them so badly that the lumber will be only second or third quality.

POULTRY HOUSES.

A GOOD poultry house is not always the one that costs the most money; in fact, as a rule, a very elaborate house is liable to be too tight to be healthy. Poultry need fresh air, and cannot be kept with any profit without it. While it is important to keep out both snow and rain, a moderate degree of cold is desirable; therefore, houses built upon sound and simple principles are more healthy, and certainly more profitable, than expensive, tight houses. The windows in the poultry house should not cover more than one quarter of the south side. When the whole south part of the house is made of glass, it is too hot when the sun shines, and too cold during cold winter nights; the hens suffer by the extreme and sudden changes of temperature.

The foundation of a house should be well constructed; the sills should be set on stone laid in cement, and the floor of the house should be covered three inches in depth with good Portland cement; thus making it proof against the entrance of rats or skunks.

GROWING POTATOES BY LEVEL CULTURE.

THERE are yet too many farmers who cling to the old custom of hilling potatoes, and are unwilling to believe that potatoes can be prevented from growing out of ground with level culture; when the fact is that not half as many potatoes will grow above the surface of the ground by level culture as by hilling the earth around the growing potatoes.

It is natural for the potato plant to extend roots on which the tubers are to grow, about two inches below the surface of the ground; and if the farmer, after these have started, should cover them two or three inches deeper by drawing up the earth around the tops, a new set of roots would grow as much above the others as their depth had been increased; thus bringing them above the depression which the farmer has made between the rows to get earth to hill up his potatoes with. When the potatoes on the upper set of roots are half grown, the earth of which the hill is made will have settled down sufficiently to expose some of the growing potatoes; and if the season be somewhat dry, the high hills will be so dry that the potatoes will cease to grow when too small to be of any value except to feed to farm stock. When the hills get dried through, the heaviest showers fail to wet them, because the water settles directly in the depressions between the hills.

In level culture the potatoes should be planted about four inches below the surface, and covered about two inches, leaving a depression to be leveled when the plants are about four inches high; when the land is thus leveled, it should be kept so during the remainder of the season. By this practice, the potatoes will grow beneath the surface of the ground, and the dry weather will injure them but very little.

When wet land is to be planted with potatoes, as they cannot be planted deep, it is necessary to hill some; but in doing so, the hill should be made broad and flat on top, leaving the depressions between the rows quite narrow.

NEW CROPS.

THE farmer should ever be on the lookout for new crops which promise to give him a good profit over their cost; but he should be cautious about adopting new things simply because they are new.

MUCK AS AN ABSORBENT.

WHEN muck is properly treated it is one of the best absorbents within easy reach of the farmer. To have it in the best condition it should be dug out two or three years before it is wanted for use and spread two or three feet deep over a level piece of land where the spading or disk harrow can be run over it often enough to prevent any vegetation from growing. In this way the air will be let in, so that by the second year the muck will become fine enough, and free enough of acid, to use the best of it. It is good economy for the farmer to keep a three years' stock of muck on hand.

POST OFFICE REGULATIONS.

(Prepared September, 1899, at the Post Office, Boston.)

DOMESTIC.

NOTE.—*All kinds of mail matter (except regular publications sent to subscribers) must be prepaid by postage stamps.*

First Class Matter.
LETTERS AND POSTAL CARDS IN THE U.S.

Letters. (To be sent beyond the office where deposited, or for any letter-carrier office). Letters and written matter, also all articles sealed, for *each ounce or fraction thereof*, no limit to weight. but if over 4 lbs. must be fully prepaid 02

Drop or Local Letters. (To be sent within the delivery of the office where deposited, if not a letter-carrier office), *for each ounce or fraction* 01

Registered Letters. The fee for registered letters (in addition to the regular postage, which must be fully prepaid) is, *per letter* 08

Postal Cards, with *no writing on the face but the address,* cost each 01

Special (or Immediate) Delivery Letters. They require a special stamp, in addition to regular postage 10

Second Class Matter (*Rates for Publishers, etc.*)

All Newspapers and other Periodicals, one copy to each actual subscriber residing within the county where they are printed, wholly or in part, and published, except those deliverable at letter-carrier offices . . . . free.

Newspapers and Periodicals to regular subscribers, and sample copies, *each pound or fraction* 01

Newspapers (except weeklies) **and Periodicals** not exceeding two ounces in weight, when deposited in a letter-carrier office for delivery by its carrier, each 01

Periodicals over two ounces in weight, prepaid by postage stamps affixed, .02

Weeklies, deliverable by carriers, at letter-carrier offices, *for each pound or fraction* 01

Transient Newspapers and Periodicals, when posted by persons other than the publisher or news agent, printed regularly in known offices of publication, for *each four ounces or fraction* 01

Third Class Matter.
MISCELLANEOUS PRINTED MATTER, ETC., IN THE U.S.

Pamphlets, occasional publications, proof-sheets, or corrected proofs, and manuscript copy accompanying the same, and all matter wholly in print not issued regularly, *in which the printing forms the principal use,* and not exceeding four pounds in weight, for *each two ounces or fraction* 01

Books (only printed). For *each two ounces or fraction,* not over four pounds in weight (*single volumes* may be over) 01

Fourth Class Matter.
MERCHANDISE IN THE U.S.

Merchandise. Samples of metals, ores, minerals, or merchandise, paintings in oil or water, crayon drawings, printed envelopes, bill-heads, letter-heads, blotting-paper with printed advertisements thereon, blank cards, photograph albums, blank books, labels, tags, playing cards; and any articles not of the other classes, and not liable to damage the mails, or injure any person, not exceeding four pounds in weight, for *each ounce or fraction thereof* 01

Seeds, cuttings, bulbs, roots, and scions, *for each two ounces or fraction.* . . .01

Fee for registration, in addition to the postage, for each package 08

UNITED STATES MONEY ORDERS.

United States Money Orders, not exceeding $100 on one order, are issued on payment of the following fees:—

Not exceeding $2.50	.03	Exc'g $30.00 and not exc'g $40.00.	.15
Exc'g $2.50 and not exc'g $5.00.	.05	Exc'g $40.00 and not exc'g $50.00.	.18
Exc'g $5.00 and not exc'g $10.00.	.08	Exc'g $50.00 and not exc'g $60.00.	.20
Exc'g $10.00 and not exc'g $20.00.	.10	Exc'g $60.00 and not exc'g $75.00.	.25
Exc'g $20.00 and not exc'g $30.00.	.12	Exc'g $75.00 and not exc'g $100.00.	.30

FOREIGN.

The rates for the countries and places, a *list of which is given below*, are as follows:—

Prepayment optional, except for registered articles, but on printed matter and samples postage must be at least partially prepaid.

Letters. **5 cents per 15 grammes,** a weight very slightly over one half ounce.

Post Cards. **2 cents each.**

Printed Matter. **1 cent for each two ounces** or fraction. Limit of weight 4 lbs. 6 oz.

Commercial Papers (Insurance Documents, Way Bills, Invoices, Papers of Legal Procedure, Manuscripts of Works, etc.) The same as for printed matter, but the lowest charge is 5 cents.

Samples of Merchandise. The rate is the same as for printed matter, but the lowest charge is 2 cents. Limit of weight 8¾ oz., except to the following countries, to which the limit of weight is 12 oz. Great Britain, France, Belgium, Ireland, Italy, Egypt, Austria-Hungary, Hawaii, the Argentine Republic, Holland, Netherlands, Newfoundland, New Zealand, Salvador and Switzerland, British Colonies in America: Bahamas, Barbadoes, Bermuda, Falkland Islands, Guiana, British Honduras, British Jamaica, Trinidad and Turks Island. Leeward Islands: Antigua, Dominica (Island of), Montserrat, Nevis, St. Christopher or St. Kitts and Tortola. Windward Islands: Grenada, St. Lucia, St. Vincent and Tobago. British Colonies in Europe: Gibraltar and Malta. British Colonies in Asia: Borneo, Ceylon, Cyprus, Hong Kong, Labuan, Straits Settlements. British Colonies in Africa: Cape Colony, Gambia, Gold Coast, Lagos, Mauritius, Natal, Seychelles Isles, Sierra Leone and St. Helena.

MDSE. for Cuba, and **Philippine Islands,** is subject to domestic rates of postage. Mail matter of all classes for persons connected with the Military or Naval forces in Cuba, Phillippine Islands and Hawaiian Islands, and all mail matter for Porto Rico, is subject to domestic rates and conditions.

Principal Countries in the Postal Union.

Africa.	Corea.	Italy.	Roumania.
Argentine Rep.	Costa Rica.	Jamaica.	Russia.
Ascension.	Cuba.	Japan.	Salvador.
Aust. Hungary.	Danish Col.	Liberia.	Sandwich Isl.
Bahamas.	Denmark.	Madagascar.	Servia.
Barbadoes.	Dominican Rep.	Mauritius.	Shanghai.
Belgium.	Ecuador.	Mexico.	Siam.
Bermudas.	Egypt.	Montenegro.	So. Australia.
Bolivia.	Falkland Isl.	Natal.	Spain.
Brazil.	Fiji Islands.	Navigator's Isl.	Spanish Col.
British Colony	France.	Netherlands.	St. Helena.
of N. Borneo.	French Col.	Netherland Col.	Straits Settle-
British E. Afr.	Germany.	Newfoundland.	ments.
British W. Afr.	Gibraltar.	New Guinea.	St. Vincent.
British W. Ind.	Great Britain.	New So. Wales.	Sweden.
British Guiana.	Greece.	New Zealand.	Switzerland.
Brit. Honduras.	Greenland.	Nicaragua.	Tasmania.
British India.	Guatemala.	Norway.	Transvaal.
Bulgaria.	Hawaii.	Orange Free State.	Trinidad.
Canada.	Hayti.	Paraguay.	Turkey.
Ceylon.	Heligoland.	Persia.	Uruguay.
Chili.	Honduras.	Peru.	Venezuela.
China, via Br. Mail.	Hong Kong.	Portugal.	Victoria.
Colombia.	Iceland.	Portuguese Col.	West Australia.
Congo.	Ireland.	Queensland.	Zanzibar.

To Canada, comprising *Brit. Columbia, Manitoba, New Brunswick, Nova Scotia,* and *Prince Edward Island,* the postage for letters, printed matter, merchandise, etc., is the same as in the United States. All matter for Canada must be fully prepaid, except letters, which must be prepaid at least 2 cents.

Parcels Post to Jamaica, British Honduras, Bahamas, Mexico, Colombia, Salvador, Caicos Islands, Rep. of Honduras, Turks Island, British Guiana, Costa Rica, Hawaiian and Leeward Islands, Barbadoes, Danish West Indies, Newfoundland and Windward Islands, not exceeding one pound, 12c.; each additional pound or fraction, 12c.

To Mexico. First class and third class postage is the same as in the United States. Merchandise can only be sent to Mexico by parcels post, and must not be sealed.

All mail matter may be registered to the above places, except parcel post packages to Barbadoes, Caicos Islands, Rep. of Honduras, Turks Island and British Guiana.

International Money Orders.

For sums not exceeding $10 . . 10c. | For each additional $10 . . . . 10c
To Great Britain, Jamaica, Cape Colony, British Guiana, and Bermuda, the limit of a single order is $50; to all other countries, $100.
There is no limit to the number of International orders that may be issued in a day.

USEFUL HINTS.

Iron pillowslips lengthwise instead of crosswise if .you wish to iron wrinkles out instead of in.

Save soapsuds if you have a garden, for they form a very useful manure for flowers, as well as shrubs and vegetables. It is well to have a sunk tub in every garden where the soapy water can stand till required for watering.

Do not give sick people fried foods or anything highly seasoned. Avoid hot bread and biscuits and strong tea and coffee.

Bathe the face and hands of a feverish person with warm water that has a bit of common soda dissolved in it. A few drops of alcohol or cologne is often pleasant to use to bathe the sick.

A nurse should use care that no person having wet or even damp clothing should enter the sick room. Never get out of patience with the whims of an invalid, but try to coax and soothe without irritating him.

Marble washstands and mantelpieces can be cleansed by simply washing the surface with warm water, to which a little borax has been added, polishing afterward with a dry cloth.

To take stains off the fingers, keep a piece of cut lemon on your wash stand and rub the spot with this previous to wetting. If this is not successful, try a piece of pumice soap. Even the pulp of a lemon, which has had the juice taken from it, is useful for this purpose.

Do not allow paint to be cleaned with soap or soda. Ammonia is far better. Use one tablespoon to every gallon of water required to clean the woodwork.

For use in polishing knives a good device is formed of two flat pieces of material, having polishing cushions on their opposing faces, the upper member being pivoted on the lower to admit the knife blade between the two.

To keep tortoise shell bright the best polish is rouge powder, used for brightening silver. If thus treated regularly no tortoise shell, however old, need look dull, as is so often the case.

New flatirons should be allowed to stand on the stove some time before using, in order to get off the coating of black. When they are rusted they may be cleaned with fine scouring soap, and when stored away for any length of time kerosene or vaseline should be put over them.

A good substitute for suet in puddings may be found in well clarified dripping if a little soaked, finely-crushed tapioca be added to the mixture.

A very young housekeeper frequently makes the mistake of planning for a great variety of dishes when she might for the same outlay have the very best cuts of meat and an abundance of the substantials.

To polish oilcloth, shred half an ounce of beeswax into a saucer, cover it with turpentine, and place it in the oven until melted ; after washing the oilcloth thoroughly, rub the whole surface lightly with a flannel dipped in the wax and turpentine, then rub with a dry cloth.

House cleaning should have no fixed date, but should depend entirely upon the weather. It is rarely warm enough to leave off fires until late in the spring, but many small things can be done before the real cleaning begins.

Steel kept in quicklime will not rust. The best thing for cleaning it is unslacked lime, but care should be used, as it may affect the eyes.

Tansy leaves scattered around spots infested by ants, will cause them to disappear.

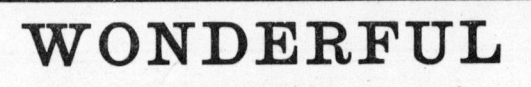